by JAY HALEY
(as author, coauthor, editor)

Ordeal Therapy

Unusual Ways
to Change Behavior

Jay Haley

Ordeal Therapy

Jossey-Bass Publishers
San Francisco • Washington • London • 1984

ORDEAL THERAPY
Unusual Ways to Change Behavior
by Jay Haley

Copyright © 1984 by: Jossey-Bass Inc., Publishers
433 California Street
San Francisco, California 94104
&
Jossey-Bass Limited
28 Banner Street
London EC1Y 8QE

Library of Congress Cataloging in Publication Data

Haley, Jay.
  Ordeal therapy.

  Includes index.
  1. Psychotherapy. 2. Family psychotherapy.
3. Psychotherapy, Brief. I. Title.
RC480.H26 1984   616.89'14   83-49252
ISBN 0-87589-595-6

Manufactured in the United States of America

The paper in this book meets the guidelines for
permanence and durability of the Committee on
Production Guidelines for Book Longevity of the
Council on Library Resources.

JACKET DESIGN BY WILLI BAUM

FIRST EDITION
    First printing: March 1984
    Second printing: September 1984

Code 8407

The Jossey-Bass
Social and Behavioral Science Series

To Cloé

Preface

This is a book about the absurd dilemmas people find themselves in and the absurd solutions offered them in therapy. The reports are accurate descriptions of actual cases. When the dialogue is lengthy, it is based on verbatim audio- and video-recordings. A piece of fiction is included as an epilogue, but even that story is based on an actual case. It was planned to be one of a series of stories, and it is reprinted here with the permission of *Voices*, where it first appeared.

I wish to thank the therapists I supervised in these situations for allowing me to present their work here. The therapy was usually done in one-way-mirror rooms with live supervision; some of the therapists were in training, and others were colleagues I was assisting. I also wish to thank the families and individuals who experienced the therapy; they have been carefully disguised to protect their anonymity.

Bethesda, Maryland   Jay Haley
January 1984

Contents

Ordeal Therapy

Unusual Ways
to Change Behavior

Introduction

One day a man, an attorney, came to me for help because he could not sleep at night. His insomnia was beginning to cost him his career because he was falling asleep in the courtroom. Even with heavy medication he was sleeping less than an hour or two each night. I had just begun private practice, and the man was sent to me to be hypnotized to solve his sleep problem. He was not a good hypnotic subject. In fact, he responded to suggestions for hypnosis just as he did when trying to sleep: He would suddenly rouse up wide awake and alert as if frightened by some thought he could not describe. After several tries, I decided hypnosis would not be the way to influence this man's sleeping problem. Yet I felt I had to do something. He'd been through traditional therapy, and nothing had helped him with his problem, which was getting progressively worse to the point that he feared he would become unable to function.

The attorney insisted that nothing was wrong with him or his life; he was happy with his work and with his wife and children. His only problem was that he couldn't sleep. As he put it, "When I start to go to sleep, something pulls me awake, and then I lie there for hours."

Finally, I tried an experiment. I suggested that at bedtime he create a pleasant situation, with his wife bringing him warm milk, as she had before. Then when he lay down to sleep, he must deliberately think of all the most horrible things he might think about or might do or see himself doing. I asked him to practice, in the interview with me, thinking of those awful things, and he couldn't think of any. When I had him think of all the horrible things a hypothetical person, "Mr. Smith," might have on his mind, however, he thought of murder, homosexual acts, and other exciting things like that. I told him that he was to lie down to go to sleep that night, but instead of trying to go to sleep, he should deliberately think of all the horrible things he could bring to mind. As he was leaving the office, he said, "You mean things like putting my wife in a whorehouse?" I said, "That's a good one."

The man went home and followed the instructions. He fell asleep immediately and slept the night through. From that point on, he used that procedure, and he lost his insomnia.

At that time, during the 1950s, there was no therapeutic theory to explain the creation of such an intervention or its success. The only theory was the psychodynamic theory of repression, which would have assumed that telling the man to think awful things would keep the man awake rather than put him to sleep, since it would mean bringing repressed material near consciousness.

At that time there was also no explanation of a rapid therapeutic change because there was no theory of brief therapy. It was assumed that if one did brief therapy, one merely did less than was done in long-term therapy. Therefore, my directive had no rationale. As I puzzled over why that case and similar ones were successful, I decided I should go and consult Milton H. Erickson.

I had learned hypnosis from Dr. Erickson, and I had talked with him about hypnosis as part of a research investigation. Finally I had begun teaching classes in hypnosis myself to local physicians and psychologists. When I went into practice as a therapist, I realized at once that hypnosis in research and teaching was not relevant to hypnosis used clinically. I knew how to give people hypnotic experiences, how to provide deep trance phenomena, and how to talk with them in metaphors about their problems. But I really didn't know how to use hypnosis to change anyone.

At that time Milton Erickson was the only consultant available to me who knew something about the use of hypnosis in brief therapy. I was also aware that he had a variety of brief therapy techniques not using hypnosis. These had come up incidentally in conversations about other matters. Actually, he was the only person I knew who was offering anything new in therapeutic technique or theory.

When I consulted with Dr. Erickson, I discovered that he had routine procedures using special ordeals to cause a change and that they were similar to the one I had devised for the attorney. I also found explanations and ways of thinking about other cases that puzzled me. For example, I had been curing a woman's severe headaches by encouraging her to have the headaches as a way to get control of them. As I talked with Erickson, I realized that his therapeutic techniques included paradoxical interventions of just that kind.

Let me present in Dr. Erickson's own words an ordeal procedure for an insomnia case he described to me:

> I had a sixty-five-year-old man come to me who had suffered a little insomnia fifteen years previously, and his physician gave him sodium amytal. Three months previously his wife had died, leaving him alone living with his unmarried son. The man had been regularly taking fifteen capsules, three grains each—a dosage of forty-five grains of sodium amytal. He went to bed at eight o'clock, rolled and tossed until midnight, and then he would take his fifteen capsules, forty-five grains, a couple of glasses of water, lie down, and get about an hour and a half to two hours' sleep. Then he

would rouse up and roll and toss until getting-up time. The fifteen capsules no longer worked since his wife died. He had gone to the family physician and asked for a prescription for eighteen capsules. The family physician got frightened and apologized for ever allowing him to become a barbiturate addict. He sent him to me.

I asked the old man if he really wanted to get over his insomnia—if he really wanted to get over his drug addiction. He said he did, and he was very honest and very sincere. I told him he could do it easily. In taking his history I had learned that he lived in a large house with hardwood floors. He did most of the cooking and the dishwashing, while the son did the housework—especially the waxing of the floors, which the old man hated. He hated the smell of floor wax, and the son did not mind. So I explained to the old man that I could cure him, that it would cost him at the most eight hours' sleep, and that's all—which would be a small price to pay. Would he willingly give up eight hours' sleep to recover from his insomnia? The old man promised me he would. I told him that it would mean work, and he agreed that he could do the work.

I explained to him that instead of going to bed that night at eight o'clock he was to get out the can of floor wax and some rags. "It will only cost you one hour and a half of sleep, or two hours at the most, and you start polishing those floors. You'll hate it, you'll hate me; you won't think well of me as the hours drag along. But you polish those hardwood floors all night long, and go to your job the next morning at eight o'clock. Stop polishing the floor at seven o'clock, which will give you a whole hour for rising. The next night at eight o'clock, get up and wax the floor. You'll really polish those floors all over again, and you won't like it. But you'll lose at most two hours of sleep. The third night, do the same, and the fourth night, do the same." He polished those floors the first night, the second night, and the third night. The fourth night he said, "I'm so weary following that crazy psychiatrist's orders, but I suppose I might as well." He'd lost six hours of sleep; he had two more to lose before I cured him, really. He said to himself, "I think I'll lie down in bed and rest my eyes for half an hour." He woke up at seven o'clock the next morning. That night he was confronted with a dilemma. Should he go to bed when he still owed me two hours of sleep? He reached a compromise. He'd get ready for bed and get out the floor wax and the polishing rags at eight o'clock. If he could read 8:15 on the clock, he would get up and polish the floors all night.

A year later he told me he had been sleeping every night. In fact, he said, "You know, I don't dare suffer from insomnia. I look at that clock and I say, 'If I'm awake in fifteen minutes, I've got to polish the floors all night, and I mean it, too!'" You know, the old man would do anything to get out of polishing the floors—even sleep.

When Dr. Erickson described that case to me, I realized at once that the procedure I had developed for the attorney was formally the same. I had arranged that the attorney go through an ordeal that he'd rather avoid by sleeping. Dr. Erickson had given his client a task that he'd rather sleep than carry out. Here was a procedure based on a rather simple premise: If one makes it more difficult for a person to have a symptom than to give it up, the person will give up the symptom. Over the years I have made use of this type of intervention in a variety of ways, and in this book I will describe the range of variations.

The ordeal process is different from some of the other therapeutic techniques originated by Milton Erickson. His use of metaphor, for example, when he would change "A" by emphasizing "B" in an analogous way, is not an ordeal procedure. In some uses of the metaphoric approach little is directly asked of the client except to listen. Similarly, Erickson's cumulation of change procedures is quite different from providing an ordeal. A person who is asked to give up pain for a second, and then to increase that to two seconds, and then to four, is going through a geometrical progression toward improvement in which no ordeal seems to be involved.

If we examine Dr. Erickson's innovations in the use of paradox, we can note that he had a person experience a distressing symptom deliberately, and that is not an ordeal procedure. Or is it? Doesn't it fall into the category of giving up a symptom to avoid an ordeal? It appears possible that ordeal therapy is not merely a technique but a theory of change that applies to a variety of supposedly different therapeutic techniques. Before proceeding further with this notion, it might be best to describe the variety of ordeal procedures and their stages.

The Ordeal Technique

With the ordeal technique, the therapist's task is easily defined: It is to impose an ordeal appropriate to the problem of the person who wants to change, an ordeal more severe than the problem. The main requirement of an ordeal is that it cause distress equal to or greater than that caused by the symptom, just as a punishment should fit the crime. Usually, if an ordeal isn't severe enough to extinguish the symptom, it can be increased in magnitude until it is. It is also best if the ordeal is good for the person. Doing what's good for you is hard for anyone and seems particularly difficult for people who seek therapy. Examples of what's good for people are exercise, improving the mind, eating a healthy diet, and other self-improvement activities. Such ordeals may also include making a sacrifice for others.

The ordeal must have another characteristic: It must be something the person *can* do and something the person cannot legitimately object to. That is, it must be of such a nature that the therapist can easily say, "This won't violate any of your moral standards and is something you *can* do." There is one final characteristic of a therapeutic ordeal: It should not harm the person or anyone else.

Given these characteristics, the ordeal offered might be crude, like a blunt instrument, or ingenious and subtle. It may also be a standard one that can be applied to many problems. Or it may be carefully designed for a particular person or family and not be appropriate for any other. An example of a standard ordeal is to exercise in the middle of the night whenever the symptom has occurred that day. An example of an ordeal designed for a particular person would require too lengthy a description here; readers will find many individually tailored examples throughout this book.

One final aspect of the ordeal: Sometimes the person must go through it repeatedly to recover from the symptom. At other times the mere threat of an ordeal brings recovery. That is, when the therapist lays out the ordeal as a procedure and the person agrees to experience it, he or she often abandons the symptom before the ordeal even goes into effect.

Types of Ordeals

A few of the different types of ordeals can be listed with examples.

Straightforward Task. When the ordeal is a straightforward task, the therapist clarifies the problem and requires that, each time it occurs, the person go through a specific ordeal. During the interview, the therapist finds out, often without making it clear what the purpose is, what the client should do more of that would be good for him or her. A typical response is that the person should do more exercising. The therapist therefore directs the person to go through a set number of exercises each time the symptom occurs. It is often best to have these exercises occur in the middle of the night. That is, the person is asked to go to sleep with the alarm set for three o'clock in the morning and then to get up at three and do the exercising. After that, the person goes back to sleep, so the procedure is like a dream or nightmare. The exercise should be sufficient so it can be felt in the muscles the next day.

As an example, with a man who became anxious when he

spoke in public as his job required, I had him exercise each
night when he had been more anxious than he thought he
should be. The exercise needed to be severe enough so that he
could feel it in his muscles at a meeting the next day. He was
soon surprisingly calm when he stood up to speak. I learned this
from Dr. Erickson who described the procedure in the same type
of case with an emphasis on using energy. His patient

> had a ritualistic, phobic, panicky reaction to his
> television broadcast—forced panting, breathing,
> and for fifteen minutes he would stand gasping,
> and gasping, and choking, and his heart would
> pound. Then they would say, "You're on," and he
> would broadcast over TV with the greatest of ease.
> But each day he became increasingly more miser-
> able. At first it started with a minute or two; by
> the time he came to see me it was built up to fif-
> teen minutes. He was looking forward to twenty
> minutes, thirty minutes, an hour; and it was begin-
> ning to interfere with his other work at the station.
> A day after I found out what his sleeping habits
> were, I gave him that concept of so much energy.
> As you would expect, his sleeping habits were
> rather ritualistic. Always in bed at a certain hour.
> Always up at a certain hour. After I got the con-
> cept of energy pounded into his head, I pointed
> out to him, why not use up that energy that he
> spent that way? [Demonstrating panting] How
> many deep squats would it take each day? I told
> him I didn't know how much energy it would take,
> but that I thought he ought to start out with
> twenty-five (in the morning before he went to
> work), even though I thought at least a hundred
> would be requisite. But he could start out with
> twenty-five. . . . No one wants to do that. . . .
> His lame, sore legs all day long convinced him that
> he had used up plenty of energy. He had none left
> over for that [demonstrating panting]. He liked

that use of his energy. He built up his knee squats, deep squats, as a health matter to reduce his obesity. Then he began going down to the gym to exercise, and he began to enjoy that daily ritual of going to the gym.

He came back to me and said, "My trouble is recurring . . . I noticed the other day I took three or four deep breaths, and the next program I increased the number, so it is starting to build up. Now what are you going to do? Because doing the exercises won't work. I've got a lot more energy." I said, "It's a profound psychological reaction you're showing." He said, "Yes." I said, "Well, suppose we work on it at the psychological level. Now, I know your sleeping habits. You sign off at ten o'clock. You go right home. You just summarize the day to your wife, and then you go right to bed. You sleep eight hours. You're a sound sleeper. You enjoy your sleep, you're a regular sleeper. After four hours' sleep, get up and do a hundred squats." He said, "That I would really hate." I said, "Yes, you can really use up a lot of psychological energy hating that idea. How do you think you'll feel psychologically every night when you set your alarm, as you always do, realizing that you can take up a lot of psychological energy panting in front of the microphone and the television camera? You can take out an awful lot of psychological energy in two ways: . . . setting your alarm for the regular time and psychologically considering with a great deal of intensity of feeling how you don't want to get up in four hours' time to do deep squats."

That analogy worked—for a while. He came back . . . . I said, "So you have got an excess of energy." He said, "That's right." I said, "Now tell me, what has been your lifelong ambition?" He said, "To own my own home for my wife and my

child." I said, "It will really make you sweat, won't
it, to buy a home and mow the lawn?" He said,
"My wife has been after me for years, and I flatly
refused to budge, but we're buying one this month."
He's had no recurrence. He's got a home. He's got a
yard. He's using up all excess energy.

This is not only typical of Dr. Erickson's ordeal therapy
but typical of the way he created a therapeutic procedure and
then arranged that it be built into the person's natural environ-
ment so the influence would continue without therapy.

When a straightforward task is chosen, it can be whatever
individual clients say is something they should do more of to
improve themselves. A classic approach of Dr. Erickson's with
insomnia, for example, was to have the person stay up all night
reading those books he or she should have read but had put off
reading. Since clients might fall asleep if they sat in a chair to
read, Dr. Erickson would require them to stand up at the man-
tle and read all night long. With such an arrangement, clients
either sleep, which is good for them, or read the books they
should read, which is good for them. Erickson reports that a
person will say, "I'm ready if I ever have the problem again. I've
bought a whole set of Dickens." The solution gives clients confidence that they can deal with the problem if it occurs again.

Paradoxical Ordeals. The ordeal can be the symptomatic
behavior itself and so be paradoxical—defined as encouraging
the person to have the problem he or she came to the therapist
to recover from. For example, a person wishing to recover from
depression can be asked to schedule the depression at a certain
time each day. Preferably it should be a time when the person
would rather be doing something else. For example, the therapist may schedule someone to concentrate on being depressed
at a time when free of other obligations, such as just after putting the children to bed during the time when one might relax
and watch television.

It is a question whether a paradoxical intervention can be
anything but an ordeal insofar as individuals are asked to go
through what they'd rather recover from. An example is the

flooding technique in behavior therapy: A person afraid of bugs and wanting to recover from that fear is asked to experience the fear of imagining bugs crawling all over him. This type of paradoxical intervention is obviously an ordeal. Similarly, requiring a quarreling couple to quarrel, or asking a couple to go through a distressing sequence that they wish to stop, is not only paradoxical but an ordeal.

To put this matter another way, insofar as a therapeutic paradox is defined as the person's rebelling against the therapist by not doing the problem behavior, there must be an ordeal involved for the person to resist doing it.

One other relevant aspect of the paradoxical intervention is the way it involves making an involuntary act, which is the definition of a symptom, voluntary. The person must deliberately do that which he or she says can't be helped, such as eat impulsively, or avoid eating, or have aches and pains, or be anxious. When done deliberately, it is, by definition, no longer a symptom. With an ordeal arrangement, one can ask that the person repeat the symptom deliberately each time it occurs involuntarily, thus making the symptom an ordeal for having experienced the symptom. If a person has two symptoms, one can be required each time the other occurs, thereby introducing a paradoxical ordeal that is effective with two symptoms at once. For example, a person who has a particular compulsion and also suffers from extreme shyness can be required to socialize as an ordeal whenever the compulsion occurs.

The Therapist as an Ordeal. There are several classes of ordeals that are effective because of the effect on the relationship with the therapist. All ordeals are in relation to the therapist and effective because of that, but some are specifically set up to be therapist-oriented.

For example, when a therapist "reframes" an act, the message becomes the ordeal. Any act that is defined in one way by the client can be redefined in a less acceptable way by the therapist so that it is something the person doesn't like. For example, something the client describes as vengeful can be redefined as protective and encouraged by the therapist. Or an act that the client defines as independent of the therapist can be redefined as done for the therapist, thereby reframing it in such a way that the person would rather not continue it.

Another class of ordeals is the confronting techniques used by some therapists. When a therapist forces the client to face what the client would rather not face, and the client has sought out this painful experience, it can be classed as an ordeal procedure. Similarly, insight interpretations that the client doesn't like are an ordeal to experience. In such cases the therapy itself, rather than a specific act by the therapist, becomes an ordeal for a person, and the ordeal must continue as long as the person has the problem.

The fee, or any other benefit to the therapist, can be used as an ordeal by increasing it when the symptom continues or is worse, a type of ordeal some therapists like to impose.

Ordeals Involving Two or More Persons. An ordeal can be designed for one person or for a unit of any size. Milton Erickson had a series of ordeals for children's therapy in which the task was an ordeal for both parent and child. In a typical procedure, for example, a bedwetting child was required, each time his bed was wet in the morning, to practice his handwriting and improve it. His mother was to wake him at dawn each morning, and if his bed was wet, she'd get him up and help him practice his handwriting. If his bed was dry, he didn't have to—but his mother still had to get up at dawn each morning. The procedure became an ordeal for mother and child that resulted in their pride in his giving up bedwetting and improving his handwriting.

With a family, ordeals are possible that can include a couple's burying a past romantic affair by going through a ritual ordeal together that is ostensibly to make the offender suffer but is actually an ordeal for both of them. Or a whole family can be put through an ordeal when a member misbehaves.

These examples indicate a wide range of possibilities; the therapist need only provide something the person would rather give up the symptomatic behavior than do. However, a sharp distinction needs to be made between therapeutic, benevolent ordeals and those ordeals that cause a person to suffer either for the advantage of a therapist or for social control reasons. Simply to lock someone in jail when he or she steals does not fall into the category of ordeal therapy but is a method of social control. All therapists should be on guard against persecution of the public under the guise of therapy. To make it quite clear, the ordeal should be voluntary by the person and good for the person experiencing it but not necessarily for the person imposing it except insofar as there's satisfaction in successfully helping someone to change when he or she wishes to.

One must always keep clearly in mind the context of any therapeutic intervention. For example, Milton Erickson once devised a procedure in which a boy out of control was sat on by his mother as a way of helping him become less self-destructive. Later this procedure was adopted by inpatient institutions as a way the staff could force children to behave. There is a sharp distinction between a loving mother reforming a child for his benefit under a therapist's guidance and a staff getting revenge on a problem child under the guise of help.

Ordeals, whether in life as a happenstance or in therapy on purpose, do not in themselves have positive effects. Only when ordeals are used with skill are the effects positive, and skill is required in the use of this technique, as in all effective therapy. To use a knife correctly in surgery is rather different from accidentally slashing here and there with a knife while stumbling through an operating room. Similarly, to inadvertently cause a person to suffer is one thing; to arrange it deliberately is quite another.

Stages of Ordeal Therapy

As with any planned therapy, the use of an ordeal should be a step-by-step process with each stage carefully done.

1. *The problem must be defined clearly.* Since the person has a consequence, an ordeal, whenever the problem occurs, it is best to define the problem clearly. As an example, the person can be asked whether he can tell the difference between normal anxiety and the special anxiety he is coming to therapy to recover from. Everyone is anxious at times in some situations. The distinction must be clear because the ordeal will follow on the presence of abnormal anxiety only. Sometimes that distinc-

tion becomes clearer after the ordeal procedure has been suffered and the person is more serious about it. One can also use
ordeals for a general feeling of boredom or lack of well-being as
a way of driving the person into a more interesting life, but that
procedure needs to be carried out with more caution than the
more simple ordeal following on a clearly symptomatic act.

2. *The person must be committed to getting over the
problem.* If a person is to go through an ordeal, he or she must
really want to get over the problem presented. The motivation to
get over it does not always exist at the time of entering therapy. The therapist must help motivate the person to take this
kind of drastic step. Offering a benevolent concern, the therapist must bring out of the client a determination to get over
the problem. The procedures are similar to getting a person to
follow any therapeutic directive, with the additional fact that
this type of directive will be unpleasant to follow. Typically
the therapist must emphasize the gravity of the problem, out-
line the failed attempts to get over it, make it a challenge that
the client is up to facing, and emphasize that the ordeal is a
standard and usually successful procedure.

An important motivation of many clients in this situation is to be willing to go through the ordeal to prove the therapist wrong. Such people have usually tried many things to get
over their problem; and if the therapist takes a firm position
that this procedure will solve it, the client finds that hard to believe. Yet the only way the client can disprove it is by going
through the procedure. Doing that has its therapeutic effect.

One way to motivate a client is to say that there is a cure
that is guaranteed, but the client will not be told what it is until
he or she agrees in advance to do it. Sometimes clients are asked
to come back next week only if they're willing to do whatever
is asked. Intrigued at the idea that something can be done to get
over the problem, and not believing that, they are placed in a
situation where they must agree to do something to find out
what that something is. In that way they are committed to do
the task.

One should keep in mind that in most cases the ordeal is
effective *in relation to* the therapist. It is done to prove the

therapist wrong, or else recovery is fast because of the therapist. Typically, for example, if the therapist is asking the person to stay up all night and lose sleep, or get up at night and clean house for an hour, it should be emphasized that the *therapist* is not going through that ordeal. The therapist can say, "I know how hard it is to get up in the middle of the night like that, because I myself so enjoy sleeping soundly all night through." Consequently, when the person is up in the night, he or she is thinking of the therapist enjoying a night's sleep.

3. *An ordeal must be selected.* The selection of an ordeal is done by the therapist, preferably with the client's collaboration. The ordeal must be severe enough to overcome the symptom, it must be good for the person so that he benefits by doing it, it must be something he can do and will accept in terms of its propriety, and the action must be clear and not ambiguous. It should have a beginning and an end clearly established.

The ordeal procedure is most likely to be followed if the client is involved in selecting the ordeal. Once it is explained to clients that they need to do something voluntarily and then the involuntary reaction of the symptom will cease—or some similar explanation—then they will think of tasks to be done. The therapist must require that the task be good for them so they don't set off punishing themselves in unfortunate ways. If they've designed a positive task themselves, they tend to carry it out with more enthusiasm, and if it's necessary to increase the severity of the task, they respond well.

4. *The directive must be given with a rationale.* The therapist needs to give the directive clearly and precisely so there is no ambiguity. He or she must make clear that the task is to occur only with symptomatic behavior and that there is a set time for it. Exactly what is to be done must be described. If appropriate, the task must be given with a rationale that makes it seem reasonable. Generally it should be a variation on the theme that if the client does something harder on herself than the symptom, the symptom will disappear. For some people, it is best to not explain but simply to tell them to do it. This more magical approach is best for the intellectuals among the clientele who

can undo or explain away any rationale and find the whole thing not necessary.

If the ordeal is at all complex, or if there is a question about its nature, writing it down is helpful to both client and therapist.

5. *The ordeal continues until the problem is resolved.* The ordeal must be done precisely each time it should be done and must continue until the symptomatic behavior disappears. Typically the contract should be lifelong.

6. *The ordeal is in a social context.* The ordeal is a procedure that forces a change, and there are consequences to that. The therapist needs to be aware that symptoms are a reflection of a confusion in a social organization, usually a family. The existence of a symptom indicates that the hierarchy of an organization is incorrect. Therefore, when a therapist resolves a symptom in this way, he or she is forcing a change in a complex organization that was previously stabilized by the symptom. If, for example, a wife has a symptom that helps maintain her husband in a superior position as the one taking care of her, that changes rapidly when an ordeal requires the wife to abandon the symptom. She and her husband must negotiate a new relationship contract that does not include symptomatic behavior. Similarly, a man who stops drinking excessively must require his family organization to change because it is no longer adaptive to that symptom. It is best for a therapist to understand the function of a symptom in the social organization of the client. If not able to understand it, the therapist must resolve the symptom warily while watching for repercussions and changes.

It is the social changes that often lead the client to a reaction as the behavioral change occurs. Expectably, the client becomes upset, and that upset is a psychological change related to social consequences. When used correctly, an ordeal does not simply change minor behavior, the person restraining himself rather than go through the ordeal. This therapeutic approach can produce basic character changes as part of the disturbing changes that occur in the person's social organization. One sign of a basic change sometimes occurs when the client reports the experience of going out of his mind at the moment of change. Sometimes, just as the ordeal is proving effective, the client will telephone the therapist and say that something strange is happening. The therapist must reassure him that what is occurring is part of the expected change and help him through the reorganization of his life.

To summarize, symptoms have a function in an organization, and it is best if the designed ordeal takes into account the hierarchical situation of the client and his or her family. If, for example, a grandmother is siding with a child against his mother, it might be appropriate to have an ordeal procedure set up between child and grandmother to encourage more distance between them. Or if a father is abdicating his responsibilities in the family, he can become part of the ordeal procedure that would improve his child. Symptoms are adaptive to organizational structures, and with the change in a symptom the organizational structure will change.

Let me give an example that illustrates the procedures in designing an ordeal as well as the need to take the family organization into account when introducing a change. A sixteen-year-old youth recently out of a mental hospital had the distressing symptom of putting a variety of things up his behind. He would do this in the bathroom, inserting into his anus various vegetables, paper, Kleenex, and so on. He would then leave the bathroom a mess with all this material. His stepmother would have to clean it up, which she did furtively so the other children wouldn't know about his problem.

What ordeal might be appropriate for this unpleasant behavior? Not only should it be something more severe than the problem so he would abandon that behavior, but it should be good for him in some way. More than that, it should involve a change in the structure of his family organization.

What became apparent in a family interview by Margaret Clark, the therapist, was the way the stepmother was burdened by the problem, and the problems of all the children, while the father went about his business. She implied that when he had had several children to take care of after a divorce, he had married her and simply handed the children and their problems over to her. Clearly there was resentment on her part and a strain on the new marriage. The boy's problem became so severe that the parents did not have to deal with the marital issues between them; this appeared to be part of the function of the symptom.

The question was whether to arrange an ordeal with just the boy or to involve his family. It was decided to involve the family, partly because the boy did not seem motivated to get over the problem and partly to make a structural change possible so the symptom would be unnecessary. How to involve the family was the next step. It seemed logical to put the responsibility for an ordeal procedure in the hands of the father, since he should take more responsibility for solving the problem and burden his new wife less. Father and son could experience an ordeal together each time the symptom occurred. The next step was selection of an ordeal appropriate to the symptom.

The procedure decided on was as follows: Each time the boy put material up his behind and messed up the bathroom, the father would be told about it when he came home from work. The father would take the youth out into the backyard and have the young man dig a hole three feet deep and three feet wide. The boy would bury in the hole all the material that he had been messing up the bathroom with and then cover it up. The next time the symptom occurred, the behavior would be repeated, and this would continue forever.

The father methodically followed the procedure with his son, and in a few weeks the symptom stopped. It was not merely that the boy did not do it; he lost enthusiasm for it, as is typical with the use of the correct ordeal. The father, pleased with his success with the boy, began to associate more with him. The wife, pleased with her husband for solving this awful problem, became closer to him, so that the boy's misbehavior to help them became less necessary. There were other problems with this boy and his situation, so that therapy continued, but the particular symptom was promptly ended and remained gone.

This ordeal had the preferred characteristics: It involved and changed the structure of organization in the family by getting an irresponsible father involved. It was more severe than the symptom, since digging a deep hole in hard ground in the fall in the cold is not a simple task. The father had to stand in the cold with the boy until the task was done, so that his attitude toward a repetition of the symptom became more negative. The boy got exercise, which he wanted, in digging the hole. Digging the hole could be considered metaphoric, as well as paradoxical, to the symptom: He had been putting things in a hole, and he was required by the therapist to put things in a hole. So the procedure involved not only an ordeal but a metaphor, a paradox, and a family organizational change. As with most therapeutic procedures, the more an ordeal deals with various aspects of a situation, the better.

The Ordeal as a Theory of Change

Up to this point the ordeal procedure has been discussed as a therapeutic technique that can be considered one of many possible types of intervention to bring about change. If we examine the ordeal in a broader context, it appears to be more than a technique—it is actually a theory of change that encompasses many therapy techniques. Is it possible to say that all types of therapy are effective because an ordeal is explicitly or implicitly involved?

Examining other theories of change, one finds there are really not many contenders on the market. There is the insight theory in its different variations. This is based on the view that men and women are rational, and if they understand themselves, they will change. The schools of therapy based on this premise range from those that probe into unconscious processes through those that offer a rational consideration of alternatives to education of parents in dealing with problem children. Included in this school are the "emotional expression" theories, also based on the theory of repression, the central idea of this theory. Just as insight into repressed unconscious ideas is said to bring about change, so is the expression of repressed dynamic emotions, whether through insight or through primal screaming. The resistances must be "worked through" by discovering ideas and expressing buried emotions.

A second theory of change derives from learning theory and proposes that people change when the reinforcements that determine their behavior are changed. The procedures range from increasing positive reinforcements to replacing anxiety with relaxation to forcing people to change with "aversive" techniques.

A third, increasingly popular theory of change is the idea that people are participants in a homeostatic system and the governors of that system must be reset to bring about change. When reset, either by amplifying a small change or by disorganizing the system and forcing a new system, the problem behaviors of the participants will change. Most of the marital and family therapies flourish within the idea of the systems theory of change.

Theories of change of this kind have several characteristics. First of all, they can explain almost any outcome in any kind of therapy, even those of opposing theories. Enthusiastic advocates will say that the "real" cause of change is based on their theory. So an insight theorist will argue that people experiencing behavior modification procedures changed because they "really" discovered things about themselves during the experience. Similarly, the learning theorist argues that the insight schools of therapy actually change their clients' reinforcement schedules, and that is what "really" produces the change. In the same way, systems theory is broad enough so that its adherents can argue that any method of therapy "really" alters the sequences in a social system and so changes the people involved. Even the entrance of a therapist into a social system must change the sequences.

Another characteristic of theories of change is that they must be conceptualized in such a way that they cannot be disproved. It is the theory no one can disprove, like the theory of the existence of God, that has a fair chance of living forever, if there is money in it.

Can the ordeal as a theory of change meet the challenge of the other theories? Certainly it fits the criterion that it cannot be disproved. One can always argue that all people in therapy go through an ordeal. Even the most ingenious experimentalist could not set up a way of disproving the notion that any therapy is an ordeal. The mere fact that one must ask for help in order to begin therapy is an ordeal. It means that one has failed to solve one's problems and must concede that one needs help. Those who do not ask for help, but enter therapy involuntarily, demonstrate the point even more; it is an ordeal to be forced to go through therapy (and even to have to pay for what one does not want).

Once in therapy, the experience is hardly a rose garden. In the insight therapies one has the unpleasant experience of having all the unfortunate thoughts and deficiencies that one doesn't like to mention examined and dwelt on. If the person objects, the therapist is likely to argue that resistance, and working through that resistance, is expected. One must suffer the exploration of what one would rather not think about. Interpretations are always about what one is reluctant to admit. At a more elementary level, Freud (who knew an ordeal when he saw one) suggested that the fee should be a sacrifice to benefit the analysis, which is an unconscious recognition of the ordeal as the basis of analysis. Whether we examine psychodynamic orthodoxy or one of the spin-off confrontation groups where people face their innermost awfulness, the insight school clearly is based on the premise that an ordeal is basic to change.

Behavior modifiers don't force people to think about their more unpleasant thoughts; they emphasize the more positive side of reinforcements. However, the therapy experience itself often includes the tedium of being lectured on learning theory as well as having someone behave in a programmed way in response to one's intimate distress. The inhuman response to a human dilemma can be an ordeal. Of course, behavior modification also revels in aversive techniques involving explicit ordeals, such as shocking people by word or electricity when they manifest symptoms. Even apparently benign techniques that don't seem aversive, such as Joseph Wolpe's reciprocal inhibition procedure, in which clients imagine their phobic situations, are not cheerful moments. It is unpleasant and can be tedious to go through imagined scene after imagined scene of situations one fears and would rather not think about, and to pay money to do that.

Family therapy also offers ordeals, both intentional and

inadvertent. To have to come together with one's family in the presence of an expert and concede that one is a failure as a parent or a child or a spouse is an ordeal. Exploring how one participated in producing a defective member, or even acknowledging that one did so, is ordealful. Therapists using acceptance techniques are likely to advise the family to continue in their misery, as is characteristic of the Milan group. Other therapists use experiential and confronting techniques, offering unpleasant insightful interpretations to the family, thereby causing a family to hint they would rather be elsewhere. Therapists who like to have families weep together and express emotions must focus on bringing out their misery.

Obviously a sound argument can be made for the ordeal as the "real" cause of change in all contemporary therapy, whatever theories the therapists think they are following. Should we confine ourselves to therapy schools? What about other aspects of human life? One thinks of religion at once. Is not the ordeal the basic rock on which is built the Christian church? Change, or conversion, in Christianity was obviously not based on the idea that the soul is saved through wine and good cheer; rather, salvation comes through misery and suffering. It is when the Christian gives up the pleasures of sex and the grape and accepts the hair shirt that conversion has taken place. The benefits of distress are part of the basic, and curious, concept of salvation through suffering. Everywhere one turns in Christian edifices, one sees the sufferer going through his ordeal on the cross. Turning to specific procedures, in the oldest tradition of the oldest Christian church is confession—an ordeal in which one must, for the good of one's Soul, reveal to another that which one would rather not. Equally old in tradition is penance, a consequence of confession. Obviously penance is a ritualized ordeal. Like therapy ordeals, penance takes two forms —penance as a standardized task and penance designed for the peculiar sins of a particular sinner.

In passing, it might be mentioned that not only Christianity and the Western world have found their way to the ordeal. If we glance at the Eastern philosophies and religions, we see that misfortune is part of enlightenment. Not only are there

Eastern religions that emphasize accepting suffering as benefi-
cial, but Zen Buddhism, with its 700-year-old procedures for
changing people, includes specific ordeals. The Zen master is
likely to bring about enlightenment by striking students with
sticks and requiring them to respond to impossible koans. Enlightenment, like salvation and therapeutic change, has painful
steps on the way to bliss.

The other area of human life besides religion where change
takes place is in the political arena. Here we also find the ordeal.
The great revolutionary movements, such as the Communist and
Socialist movements, set out to change the masses of the world.
To achieve this change, participants in the movement are expected to make sacrifices and go through disciplined ordeals.
Every mass movement requires sacrifices and giving up the world
of pleasure for the cause. It seems evident that if an individual,
or a whole society, is asked to change, the ordeal is central to
the process of transformation.

Whether we examine the ordeal as a technique or as a
universal theory of change, its merits demand further examina-
tion and exploration. As a subject of research and training for
many years to come, it has one aspect that needs great emphasis. Like any powerful means of changing people, the ordeal is
a procedure that can cause harm in the hands of the ignorant
and irresponsible who rush off to make people suffer. More
than any other technique, it can be misused by the naive and
incompetent. We should all keep in mind that society grants
permission to therapists to impose their help on people to re-
lieve suffering, not to create it.

1

———❖———❖———❖———❖———❖———❖———❖———❖———

A Touch of Penance

She was a woman in her early thirties who looked harassed and disheveled. Obviously attractive, she had let herself go as if she didn't care. "Look," she said, and showed me her hands. They were wet with perspiration—almost dripping. "I work in an office," she said, "and every paper I touch gets wet unless I constantly dry my hands."

She said she had begun to suffer from extreme anxiety about two years previously. The form the anxiety took was regular outbursts of perspiration, particularly on her hands. She couldn't say what she was anxious about; it was just a general feeling of anxiousness that seemed to come over her for no reason. She had spent the last year in therapy with a focus on the past, particularly her childhood experiences and traumas, searching for the basis of her anxiety. The symptom continued to get worse. Finally she was referred to me because something had to be done or she would lose her job, as her wet hands dampened everything she touched. "My family needs the money," she said. "I have to work. We're far into debt, and if I lose my job,

24

we're in real trouble." She told me she had four young children and a husband. When she mentioned her husband, she said their marriage was "all right," in a way that indicated it was not. Her manner made it clear she did not want to discuss her marriage.

Talking with the woman about her life, I found it was a busy one. She not only held a full-time job but also took care of the four children, the youngest just starting school, without household help. She did the cooking and the washing and spent weekends doing the heavy cleaning. Days off, as well as vacations, were out of the question. Her husband "helped some," she said. He was a salesman and his income was "irregular." When her husband was mentioned, she changed the subject to her anxiety and its physical sensations.

A dutiful woman who seemed always to strive to do the right thing and shoulder all the burdens, she found that somehow her anxiety attacks prevented her from doing what she should. On many weekends, she said, she just had to sit and do nothing instead of doing the housework, because of the stress of the anxiety. Her house was often a mess, no matter how she tried. Her anxiety and her wet hands made everything just too difficult to do. I asked her whether there was something specific she should do more of that she wasn't doing that would make her feel better if she did it. She said that if she washed and waxed the kitchen floor more often, she would feel better. She just couldn't stand a dirty kitchen floor, yet her floor was usually that way. She also said she should do more with the children —take them more places, spend more time with them, help them with their homework. Having been raised a Catholic, she also wished to take the children to church more often but didn't feel up to it.

The woman talked about her life with some reluctance, saying that she was there for her anxiety and her wet hands, not to tell her life story. Her other therapy had been talk, talk, talk and hadn't changed anything. I took these statements as an expression of her willingness to take action and agreed that she needed a drastically different therapy. When I asked whether she was really ready to get over the problem, she said of course she was. She was ready for anything. Would she make a sacri-

fice, I asked? Of course, she said. Would she do something that
seemed strange and take my word for it that it would solve her
problem? She began to hesitate and asked what I meant by
"strange." I told her that it would be strange in the sense that it
would be different from her previous therapy. She said that that
would be fine as long as it worked.

"There is something I want you to do," I said, "and I
want you to do it exactly, with no modifications or improve-
ments of your own."

She asked what she was to do. I assured her it was something she could do, that it would not violate any moral standard, but it would be something she would not like. In fact, she
would not like it so much that she would give up her anxiety
rather than do it.

As she puzzled over this, I asked her whether she could
clearly tell when she was abnormally anxious and when she was
not. "Certainly," she said. "It's when I break out in perspiration
and my hands are wet."

"You can tell that anxiety and perspiration from normal
anxiety and sweating on a hot day?"

"Of course," she said. "There's no question."

"Fine," I said, "and do you like a good night's sleep?"

Puzzled, she replied, "Of course I like a good night's
sleep. Who doesn't?"

"Well, I am going to ask you to make a sacrifice," I said.
"You say you want to get over this problem quickly. Are you
determined to get over it?"

"Yes," she said, "I have to."

I began to talk to her about physiology. I pointed out
that the body digests food without our having to think about it
or know how it happens. The body also maintains the correct
temperature. When we're too hot, we perspire to cool the body
by the evaporation of water from the skin. Sometimes the body
is not functioning correctly, as in her case, and she perspired
from anxiety rather than because it was hot. She would therefore have to arrange that her body function correctly.

"How on earth can I do that?" she asked.

"If you follow a simple procedure, you can do that," I

said. I gave her the example of a child who learns, without knowing how, to control his sphincter so that his bladder holds in water until he goes to the bathroom. With some children, the body is malfunctioning and the sphincter releases water from the bladder while the child is in bed asleep. The task is to persuade the body to retain the water until the child goes to the bathroom. Sometimes it is necessary to have the child do something that requires the body to begin to perform correctly.

"What can be done?" she asked.

The problem, I pointed out, was to arrange that the child do something that is harder on his body than wetting the bed, and his body will gain control. For example, I pointed out to her, a seventeen-year-old boy had come to me because he wet the bed every night and had always done so. Usually the wet bed woke him up, and he'd change the sheets, climb back into the dry bed, and sleep the rest of the night. His problem was that he was about to go away to college. It was just too embarrassing to wet the bed at his age in a college dormitory, and so he wanted the problem solved. I said I could help him solve this problem himself, since he was old enough to do so. I asked him what he considered a long walk. He said he considered a mile a long walk, since he didn't exercise much. I explained to him that he needed to do something that was more difficult for him than wetting the bed. Doing that would stop the bedwetting because his body would change its physiological response and his sphincter would gain control. If he wanted fast action, he must do something that would be hard for him to do. He agreed to do what was necessary. I told him that if he wet the bed that night, he was to climb out of that wet bed, get dressed, and walk one mile. Then he was to undress and climb into the wet bed, without changing the sheets, and sleep through the night. The next night, if he awakened with a wet bed, he had to repeat the procedure. He had to do that every night until the problem was gone. He was rather shocked at the idea of walking in the night and climbing back into a wet bed, but he agreed. I added that there was always the possibility that he might not wake up in the night but might awaken in the morning with a wet bed. If so, he should set the alarm the following night for

two o'clock in the morning and get up and take the mile walk
that he owed. Thus, any night the bed was wet, he must go
through this physical act so that his body would change its responses.

The young man dutifully clocked one mile in his neighborhood that afternoon. That night, when he awakened with a
wet bed, he got up and did his mile walk. He did that regularly.
Within two weeks he was wetting the bed only occasionally, and
in a month the bedwetting had stopped.

I didn't mention to the woman that after the youth had
got over his problem, his parents had come to me and said they
had a marital problem that had increased with the possibility of
the son's going away from home. Now that he was over the bedwetting problem, he was really going to leave them. They were
not sure their marriage could continue if they no longer had a
child with them. I spent time with them resolving issues in their
marriage. The youth went to a local university and so was near-
by, but he decided not to visit home for three months to aid the
separation from his parents.

As I told the woman about that youth, she was interested, although she didn't seem to like to have her profound
anxiety compared with a bedwetting problem. As she understood the rationale behind what was going to be asked of her, I
said, "In your case, you must do something that is so hard on
you that your body will simply stop perspiring inappropriately
and begin to function well."

"Heavens," she said, "what could be harder on me than
this anxiety?"

"I know what you must do," I said, "and now that I have
your agreement to do it, I can tell you what it is." She waited
expectantly. I said, "You'll have to do something in the middle
of the night each day that you are abnormally anxious. That is
why I asked whether you could recognize the abnormal anxiety
when it happened."

"I can recognize it," she said. "In fact, I can't avoid
knowing when it happens. But what must I do in the night?"

I looked at her thoughtfully, delaying a response. "Something that will be an ordeal," I said. "Something that is also

good for you, and you will feel better for having done it. Are you ready to hear what that is?"

"I'm ready," she said grimly.

She became more grim as I outlined the procedure. Beginning the next day, if she was anxious enough to perspire abnormally, she was to set her alarm clock for two in the morning. She was not to stay up until two o'clock but to go to sleep and wake up to the alarm. When she awakened, she was to go downstairs, get out the cleaning materials, and mop the kitchen floor. She was to wait for it to dry, and then she was to put a coat of wax on the floor. When that was done to her satisfaction, she was to go to bed. The following night, if she'd been abnormally anxious during the day, she was to set the alarm and get up again. She was to wash that wax off the kitchen floor, wait for the floor to dry, and then rewax it until it was shining enough to meet her standards. This type of ordeal was especially painful because it involved wasted work: To wax a floor on one night and remove the wax the next gives a feeling of doing what is not necessary. That severe an ordeal seemed called for by the severity of the woman's problem and her situation.

I finished describing the task, said to her that I knew she was a woman of her word and would do it. Before dismissing her, I added two other factors. She was to do this until she stopped being abnormally anxious even if that meant forever. I also said kindly that as she was scrubbing the floor, she could realize that she was making a nicer home for her husband.

I made an appointment for three days later, expecting that the woman would be upset at the task and in a dilemma whether to keep following the directive as she'd promised. When she came in, she was upset, but not over having to scrub floors in the night. She was furious at her husband and wanted to talk about that. She said she could no longer stand him; he was a bum who would always be a bum. I had to inquire whether she had followed the floor-scrubbing instructions. She said she had got up the first night, since she had been anxious that day. However, she had not got up in the night and scrubbed the floor again. I thought at first she meant she'd broken her promise, but instead she meant it hadn't been necessary to go through the ordeal. She showed me her hands. They were perfectly dry, a quite astonishing physiological change. She said her anxious spells had simply disappeared, and instead she felt angry.

I complimented her on her success, but she dismissed that lightly. She said she wanted to talk about her husband rather than her anxiety. She had had enough of him and was going to leave him. She told quite an amazing story. Her husband had not supported the family for years, if ever. In fact, he made no money. He was a salesman who never sold anything. He went from product to product, being dismissed from place after place. Worse, he cost the wife money. Regularly he wrote bad checks, sometimes so bad that he didn't even have accounts in the banks he wrote the checks on. A dozen times she had had to go pay off the bad checks at stores and banks that were threatening to bring charges. Not only was her salary supporting the family, but it was being wasted saving the husband from jail and her family from embarrassment. She said she no longer intended to save him from anything. If she could get up in the night and scrub floors, he could straighten himself out or she would leave him. She'd been about to give up her job and stop supporting him—the anxiety had been forcing that—and now she decided to keep the job and get rid of the husband. Even if the children needed a father, she would throw him out rather than let him live off her labors.

At the end of the interview, I asked the woman to bring in her husband to see whether something could be done about him to save the marriage. He came in, a large, ungainly man with a sheepish smile. He looked both furtive and contrite. Apparently assuming that I was on his wife's side, he had on his best salesman manner as he shook hands and seemed ready to placate me.

I said, "I don't know what your wife has told you, but I know what she has told me. She says that you have not done what you should in the marriage and she has had to save you from jail a number of times."

"She's right," he said, "and I'm terribly sorry."

Turning to the wife, I said, "I would like you to tell your husband just what you think of him—both his deficiencies and his assets."

"I'll be glad to," said the woman. She proceeded to specify her husband's inadequacies in considerable detail. Obviously she had a great deal on her mind that she had stored up and never said frankly to him. She discussed his total inadequacy as a wage earner, his willingness to let his wife support him, and his helpless, frightened ways that forced her to do everything. She had to deal with whatever went wrong in the home or school or neighborhood. She had to take care of the house and the kids and bring in the salary while he did nothing but disappear and drink. She detailed his criminal activities in terms of each bad check he had ever written. Her description of him was an artistic performance in its devastating review of his character and behavior. The only asset she could think of was that his intentions were sometimes good and he was nice to the children. In work, life, and bed he was a failure.

The husband sat contritely, nodding his head in agreement as she outlined his deficiencies. He did not protest. He agreed with what she said. There was no reaction of anger. He behaved like a man who was scared and contrite and trying to pacify her.

I asked him whether he had anything to say about her description, and he said he had not. He only wished she wouldn't divorce him but would give him another chance. She, of course, replied that she had given him a thousand chances and was tired of his promises. However, she was less extreme in her condemnation of him, implying some room for compromise. The diatribe I had encouraged was a painful ordeal to him (and the extent of her objections seemed to surprise her), but it served the purpose of getting her past her determination to separate and allowed the possibility of change. I asked her to wait in the waiting room while I talked with her husband alone.

He pulled his chair toward me when we were alone and said, "I don't want her to divorce me."

"I don't want her to do that, either," I said.

"I'll do anything," he said. "I swear I'll never write a bad check again."

As we talked, he explained that he was realizing there was something wrong with him. He was a salesman, and yet he was afraid of people. He had great difficulty getting up his nerve to

approach someone to sell something. Often he hid out in neighborhood bars, quietly having a beer and talking with the bar-
tender, when he should have been out knocking on doors. Often
he met other salesmen hiding there. He said that he sometimes
felt so terrible about not making any money that he behaved
like a phony and pretended he was rich and wrote bad checks.
Sometimes he wrote the check because the family had to have
something and he simply didn't have the money. He said that he
was grateful to his wife for keeping him out of jail but that
really he was a failure in life. She was right in everything she
said about him. I told him that thinking that way would not
help. He would lose her. He had to do something.

"But what?" he asked.

"Something you choose to do yourself," I said. "And
you don't have much time, because she will leave you, no fool-
ing."

I asked him whether he knew anything about anything,
and he proved to know a lot in many areas because he had sold
products in so many businesses. He particularly knew automo-
biles, since he had sold, or failed to sell, them in different agencies. He also knew used cars and could judge their mechanical
condition well. Despite that knowledge, he had never made any
money selling cars. He was the salesman the agencies used as an
example of what not to do when trying to close a deal. Somehow, when he talked to people, they decided to buy a different
kind of automobile.

As we talked, I largely listened, only pointing out occasionally that his way of thinking wouldn't solve his problem.
When he became depressed and hopeless, I pointed out that it
was too late to be depressed and hopeless: That wouldn't help
him keep his wife, and he had better do something else. At the
end of the interview I brought the wife in and suggested that she
give him a short period of time to straighten himself out and
that she refuse to help him or advise him in any way. He knew
what he should do, and she shouldn't be tricked into guiding
him. She grudgingly agreed to wait to see what he would do. He
left the office in a serious and thoughtful mood.

We had set an appointment for the following week, but

the next day the husband called me and asked for an emergency appointment. He said something had happened.

When he came in, there was a different quality about him. He looked disheveled and disoriented and was extremely serious in his manner. He said his mother was visiting them that week. After the therapy interview the previous day, he had talked with her. She had told him a surprising thing—he was not her natural son but had been adopted at birth. At age thirty-four he learned for the first time that his parents were not his biological parents. He wanted to come in and talk about this because it was such a shock, and he was thinking through his past life in terms of this new knowledge. I largely listened to him as he talked about what this meant to him. He said he had always felt there was something wrong about himself. His parents had reacted to him at times in puzzling ways that made him feel uncertain. There had been something missing that he could never understand, and he had felt the world was a place with something not quite right about it. What he was expressing was an experience children often have when they are adopted and not told. There are mysterious reactions. For example, when a neighbor says the boy looks just like his father, there is a moment's hesitation or an unusual expression by the parent. If an issue of some genetic trait comes up, the parents pause before they discuss it. The man reviewed his past and said he'd always had a feeling there was some secret about him. Not knowing what it was, he vaguely thought it was something about himself that was deficient, and no one would tell him what it was. "I always felt there was something missing," he said. "I felt incomplete."

He told me that he had not slept the previous night but had lain there thinking of his life from this new perspective. He also found himself angry at his mother for not telling him sooner. When he had asked her why she had not, she said she had always meant to but somehow couldn't find the right moment. She had planned definitely to do so when his father died, but then she had decided the death was enough of a blow without adding the adoption to it. Each year that she didn't tell him made it that much harder to tell him.

I asked him why she had told him at this time, and he said he didn't know. I suggested that he must have spoken to her in some way, perhaps in a more mature and responsible way, so that she felt that now he was ready to tolerate being told.

When the couple came in together the following week, there was a surprising change. The husband said he had a few things to say and he wanted his wife to listen. In an angry but controlled manner, he said he was sick of the way he was treated by women. He didn't like the way his mother had lied to him all his life, saying he was her natural son when he wasn't. He also didn't like his wife always treating him badly. Granted he wasn't all he should be, there were objections that he wanted to express whether she threatened to leave him or not. He said he was sick and tired of a messy house and bad meals and a complaining wife. He didn't like to walk across a kitchen floor that his shoes stuck to because of the garbage on it, and he didn't like his wife sitting around being anxious on a weekend while he cleaned house. He said she had used her anxiety to avoid sex and to avoid housework. It was time she changed and became a competent and affectionate wife. When she protested that she did the best she could with her anxiety and her job and four children, he said he didn't think she did the best she could and he was sick of living in a pigpen. The wife began to argue that if he would do what he should, she could do what she should. I encouraged them to begin to negotiate a new way of living rather than attack each other. Over the next few weeks we had a number of sessions working out these issues between them. The husband got a nine-to-five job as a service manager in an automobile agency. The wife's anxiety attacks disappeared. The simple ordeal of scrubbing and waxing the kitchen floor had apparently led to an explosive chain reaction.

2

Stumping the Experts

When the woman with the problem of compulsive handwashing brought in her chart, she had washed as many as fifty-five times one day that week. "My hands were sore," she said. "I'll bet they were," said Dr. Charles Fishman. He stroked his beard thoughtfully, studying the woman and her husband. Finally he told them that if they did what he said, he would guarantee a cure of the abnormal handwashing. The couple did not believe that was possible and asked what they had to do. Dr. Fishman said he wasn't sure he should tell them.

When someone believes that nothing can be done to help her and all the experts are stumped, it's sometimes a good idea to offer a guaranteed cure. The person becomes provoked to find out what the cure is, since it is believed not to be possible. In the process of finding out, she takes the steps necessary to get over the problem. Two couples with similar problems nicely illustrate this approach. The compulsive handwasher was dealt with by Dr. Charles Fishman, a psychiatrist. A more contemporary problem, compulsive binging and vomiting, was resolved by

Robert Kirkhorn, a social worker. Not only had both clients failed in previous therapy and were sure they could not be cured, but in both cases it was a puzzle why they had such severe symptoms. Sometimes a therapist, no matter how imaginative, simply cannot come up with a theory to explain the severity and persistence of a symptom. In such cases the use of a guaranteed cure is helpful, since it is possible to use that approach whether or not one knows why a person has the problem.

It should be emphasized that the guaranteed cure offered in these situations is a specific intervention to achieve a particular goal. It is not a matter of a therapist promising to cure his or her patients when therapy begins, which would be improper (unless the therapist can actually cure them all). The guarantee is used to persuade the client to follow the directive that sets up an ordeal.

The handwasher had struggled for years trying to restrain herself from scrubbing her hands many times a day. Her hands were often red and raw. She even slept with them Vaselined inside gloves to ease them. As is typical with problems of excessive washing, she was concerned that she might in some way be contaminated with something, and so she had to wash it away. Unsure whether the washing had successfully removed the contamination, she had to wash again, and again, and again. The irrational nature of this concern, as well as the hidden wishes and fears behind it, had been explored at length in previous therapy with no results, as is typical with the therapy of this problem. The woman liked to discuss how irrational the whole thing was. As she put it, "Why do I drive in my automobile, stop for a red light, and see a man doing something on the sidewalk—then I'm compelled to go and wash my hands because I may have touched whatever he is doing? I saw a man today, and he was sprinkling something on the grass. I don't know what he was sprinkling. I have no idea. For a half hour after I saw him, I had the compulsion to wash my hands because I may have touched what he had. Yet I never got out of the car. I was nowhere near him. Had I been home, or near home, I would have turned around and gone home and washed my hands." She washed her

hands only at home because public bathrooms might be contaminated.

The woman had tried to solve her problem in many ways
and with several therapists. She had been given insight into the
problem in one therapy and had learned about her fears of contamination and how these were related to hostile wishes and to
sex. Another therapist had paradoxically encouraged her to
wash her hands, which only provoked her to increase her handwashing. All the experts failed, and over time she stopped seeing
therapists and went on washing her hands excessively.

The problem came to Dr. Fishman's attention during
therapy for a child in the family, a boy who refused to go to
school. Family therapy resolved that problem, and as the therapist was terminating, the woman mentioned she had this handwashing problem and wondered whether he might do something
about that. Dr. Fishman began a series of interviews with the
couple together, dealing with the problem by approaching it
through the couple rather than the wife alone, in contrast to her
previous therapy.

After several weeks, the handwashing was still continuing
and the therapist was uncertain what to do next. He'd tried a
number of procedures that hadn't produced a sufficient change.
One of the problems was the way the husband and wife, while
agreeing to be cooperative, never quite followed directives.
They only partially did what he said, and so there was only a
partial improvement, which ended when they stopped following the directive.

The couple were in their late thirties and had several children. The husband, an engineer, was a responsible man, always
trying to do the right thing. He was extremely patient with his
wife. The woman was attractive, with rather owlish eyes. She
had a sense of humor that even expressed itself about her handwashing problem. The couple had been having difficulties in
their marriage, which seemed to become more extreme when
their problem with their son improved. Appearing to be on the
edge of separation at that point, they sought therapy for the
handwashing. The therapist worked with them as a couple to resolve some marital difficulties as well as the handwashing. Over

the weeks, the couple's relationship improved more and more; they even began plans to buy a new house and were clearly intending to stay together. However, the excessive handwashing continued.

Dr. Fishman tried a number of procedures and ordeals for the couple in an attempt to influence the handwashing. From the first session, he had the husband keep a chart of the handwashing, noting and counting every handwash. To provide an ordeal that would make the handwashing more difficult, he had the husband and wife talk about the handwashing—and only the handwashing—every evening for an hour, on any day when she washed her hands abnormally. The couple dutifully talked about the handwashing *ad nauseam* every night, but the ordeal did not affect the handwashing. At one point the husband, who thought he should exercise more, was required to exercise when his wife washed her hands excessively. He dutifully exercised, at least for a period, with no influence on the handwashing. To determine what was a normal handwashing and what was abnormal, as well as to provide an ordeal, the couple were asked to buy distilled water, and the woman was to wash the abnormal times only in the distilled water. Her usual handwashing would be in ordinary water. She did this for a period and stopped.

Curiously, the involvement of the husband became more apparent when the therapist asked the wife to deal with the handwashing herself and to keep the chart herself for a week. She was to stop fighting her compulsion and wash her hands whenever she felt the slightest impulse. She did so, and as a result she was washing them twice as much as usual. She had been told not to tell her husband about any of the washings. When the therapist asked whether she had told her husband about it, she said she had not.

"But I had some intimation about how things were going," said the husband.

"She didn't tell you when you called home that she was going to wash her hands?" asked the therapist, checking to see whether the wife had dealt with her problem by herself.

"Yes, she did."

"Oh, that I did," said the wife, "or I showed him that I was washing my hands."

"Which I questioned," said the husband. "I said that wasn't the way she was supposed to do it."

"Yes, but I thought I was allowed to be reassured," she protested.

"No, your husband wasn't supposed to hear about it at all."

"That's what I thought," he said.

"Oh, he wasn't to reassure me? Like if I wash my hands and say, 'Hey, I'm washing my hands.' " She looked at the two men warningly and said, "I'll use the kids, then."

The therapist, who had not heard about this need of the wife for reassurance about washing her hands, inquired further into it. "What kind of reassurance do you get?"

"I just want to know that I'm washing my hands. I'll use whoever is around, like the kids, or Ralph."

"You want to know that you're washing your hands?" asked the therapist. "Could you ask your husband for reassurance now? I mean, let's pretend that you just washed."

"I'll wash my hands," the wife said, illustrating with her hands, "lather up with soap, and say, 'Hey, Ralph, look at the soap on my hands, I've washed my hands.' I'll go rinse them, dry them, and say, 'Did I wash my hands?' He'll say, 'Yes, you washed your hands.' "

"I see," the therapist said.

"Sometimes he gets annoyed."

"Really?"

The wife turned to her husband. "This week you were a little annoyed because it happened so often."

"Yes, it was often this week."

The therapist said, "Yes, fifty-five times one day. I'm not clear what type of reassurance you want?"

"I just want to be sure that I've washed my hands. You know, that type of reassurance."

"Well, why don't you know?"

"Somehow I don't know. I do know, but I don't know, if you know what I mean."

Describing the reassurance further, the woman said that she would call her husband at the office while washing her hands and ask him whether she was doing so, and he would dutifully say that she was, and so she would be reassured. Although it could be considered irrational of the woman to wash her hands so often, it was equally irrational of the husband to reassure her that she had indeed washed her hands. She also reported that if she was afraid she had touched something, when clearly she had not, she would ask her husband whether she had touched it. He would reassure her that she had not. Talking about this, the husband imitated mock anger, saying, "Sometimes I say, 'No, you didn't touch it!' "

"You don't grab her or shake her or anything?" asked the therapist.

"I grab her sometimes, but that's another topic," the husband said, implying affectionate grabbing. The couple had previously discussed their sexual relations and reported them to be satisfactory.

When the therapist asked the couple how their life would be different if the wife stopped washing her hands abnormally, they said it would not be. As the husband put it, "She would be like she was before, except she would not wash her hands so much." The therapist asked them whether, if that occurred, they would take a vacation alone together to celebrate getting over the problem. They said it was unlikely that they would go off anywhere without the kids.

"Well," Dr. Fishman said, "I have a plan that will stop the handwashing, but I don't know what good it would be if your life is just going to be the same when she is over the problem. I don't know if you even want to hear about this plan."

This guaranteed cure procedure, the "shaggy dog" technique, was devised by Milton H. Erickson. It is called that because the therapist, after offering a cure, delays telling the couple what it is and talks about other things. He talks on and on about this and that until the couple become desperate to hear what the cure is. They become motivated to do what they are told because they become so invested in trying to find out what they are to be told to do.

When Dr. Fishman said he wasn't sure they'd even want to hear about the plan, the wife said, "Sure, I want to hear about it."

"Let's hear it, let's hear it," said the husband.

"Well," the therapist said, and then was silent for a few moments. "I'm not going to tell you about it until you agree to do it."

"Agree to do what?" the wife asked.

"This is something you *can* do so that Sarah will stop the handwashing."

"You want me to agree to something when I don't know what I'm agreeing to?" asked the husband.

"If you want to hear about it; otherwise just—"

"I'll agree," said the husband.

"Because it's not going to be easy for you." He looked at them thoughtfully. "You want to talk it over?"

"Talk what over?" asked the wife.

"I agree," the husband said.

"Well," said the therapist, "you might both talk it over."

"Talk what over?"

"Because maybe Sarah doesn't want to get over it."

"Yes, I want to get over it."

In this procedure, clients are asked to agree in advance to do whatever is asked. They must be committed to doing the task before they're told what it is. If they simply agree at once to do anything, they are not taking the task seriously and are likely to not do it or to half do it. Sometimes it is best to put off telling them for a week until they have thought it over. The therapist can say, "Come back next week only if you agree to do anything I say."

To agree to do something without knowing what it is will arouse ideas of all kinds in the client. Sometimes these are sexual ideas, sometimes other kinds pertinent to that particular client. The issue of trust in the therapist is central in this procedure.

If the client begins to say he will do anything except something that violates his moral standards, or anything except harming someone, then the therapist knows he is taking the task seriously and becoming ready to do what he must.

The therapist began to talk about other things. He asked the couple about their social life, and they discussed a dance they had gone to on Saturday night. Finally he returned to the topic and said, "It's been a long road."

"We've tried everything imaginable," said the wife.

"Well," the therapist said, "you haven't tried the one thing that I have in mind. But it's going to take a commitment from you. You're going to have to agree to do it, or I'm not going to tell you what it is. Both of you are going to have to agree."

"I mean, what are we here for, you know?" asked the husband, getting irritated. "I want to hear what you have to say."

"It's not a question of hearing what I have to say," said the therapist, looking stern. "It's a question of doing it. Because there have been lots of things I've had to say . . ."

"It's not going to hurt me, is it?" the husband asked, jokingly.

"There have been lots of things that I've said that no one did."

"That's not true," said the husband.

"For example, the distilled water," the therapist said, referring to the directive to do abnormal handwashing only in distilled water. "You must have dozens of bottles of distilled water there unopened."

"One," said the woman.

"You know you don't do all the things I say, and I'm not going to tell you this until you both agree to it." After a pause he added, "Really, solemnly agree. Because I know you're both people of your word."

The emphasis on the clients' being people of their word is often helpful in the commitment to the task. To give one's word and then not follow the directive is improper. Sometimes it helps to emphasize the religious background of a couple in this situation so that the church is called on as witness to their keeping their word.

"Is it difficult?" the wife asked after a pause.

"I'm not going to tell you until you agree. Because you really have to be agreed to do this, and promise to do this, or I'm not going to tell you what it is." He stood up and added, "I'll be back in a minute." Leaving the room, he went behind the one-way mirror to consult with the supervisor while the couple remained alone in the room discussing the task.

"The suspense mounts," said the husband, chuckling.

After a pause, the wife said, "Do you agree to do whatever it is?"

"Certainly," said the husband.

"No qualms?"

"Except to have me shoot myself," he laughed. "Cause bodily harm."

"Solemnly swear," the wife said, "to tell the whole truth and nothing but the truth, so help you God?" She laughed. "So you'll do whatever he says, even if it's difficult?"

"I've done many difficult things," he said, and added thoughtfully, "No, not really."

"Not too difficult." After a pause, she said, "It would be worthwhile, right? Does it cost any money?"

"It's a guarantee," said the husband.

"Hmm?"

"This is a guaranteed thing."

"Guaranteed?"

"That's what he said."

"I find that hard to believe," she said, laughing. "I'm a skeptic, I don't know. I'm willing to try—to do, not to try."

It is the idea of a "guaranteed" cure that most incites a client to agree to follow an unknown directive. She has usually tried everything to get over a symptom and simply cannot believe that a therapist can tell her to do something that will guarantee she will get over the problem. Clients get covertly angry at such a statement of guarantee and want to prove the therapist wrong. Yet there is only one way they can prove the therapist wrong—by doing the task that is guaranteed to cure them and then not being cured. However, to do the task, they must first find out what the task is. They therefore have to commit themselves to doing it in order to disprove the therapist.

After a while the therapist returned to the room and picked up the handwashing chart. Previously he had complimented the husband on his chart. Now the wife said, "You can tell me what a lovely chart I make."

"It's beautiful," the therapist said. "It's really—I'm very

impressed with the way you recorded these. These are all abnormal, right?"

"Yes," said the wife.

"The way you recognize abnormal handwashings," the therapist said admiringly. He emphasized this because the task he would give them would require them to distinguish normal from abnormal handwashings, and so it was important that she be able to make that distinction.

"I had to make two graphs," said the wife. "I had to change the scale. My first scale wasn't large enough."

"It's very, very nice. Realistic, not overly optimistic, not pessimistic." He put down the chart and said, "Okay, did you have a chance to talk about this?"

"It's guaranteed," said the husband.

"But it won't be easy," the therapist said.

"Guaranteed," repeated the husband.

"Yes," the therapist said.

"I'm a skeptic," said the wife.

"You both have to agree."

"We agree," said the wife. "Provided we don't have to go and shoot ourselves or anything like that."

"Break a leg or something," said the husband. "Make me take two days off from work."

"You wouldn't object to that, would you?" she asked.

"Well, I think you're being too light about this," said the therapist. "This is serious. You know, we've been working here a long time, and I've made a lot of suggestions that nobody has followed."

"That's not an accurate statement," the husband said.

"Well," the therapist pointed to the chart, "were these with distilled water or regular?"

"Regular," the wife said. "We'd be broke if those were with distilled water."

"Some things, yes, we haven't followed, but . . ." said the husband.

"Okay, I'll accept that," said the therapist. "So what do you think?"

"Yes," said the wife.

"I mean, you know, if this stops—or when this stops—you're liable to feel a little upset."

"Why would I get upset?"

"Because you'll be losing something that's part of you."

"That would be like losing ten pounds," laughed the woman. "I wouldn't be upset over that."

All were quiet. After a while the therapist said, "So what do you think? Did you have a chance to talk about it?"

"Yes," the husband said.

"What did you decide?"

"Let's hear it," he said.

"We'll do it," said the wife.

"You'll both do it?" the therapist asked.

"Yes," said the husband.

The therapist was thoughtful. "That means you'll do it," he said to the husband. "And you'll do it," he said to the wife.

"Yes," the wife said.

"And it won't be easy," said the therapist.

"It's guaranteed, right?" the wife asked.

"It's guaranteed."

"Even if it's not guaranteed, we'll do it," said the husband.

"Right," said the wife, "I'll try anything."

"Well, it's guaranteed. It will work. But you know, you don't have to agree this week. If you want to put it off a week." They laughed and he added, "I'm serious. I don't want you to rush into it."

The husband said, "Why not tell us and give us a chance to think about it?"

"Do you want to talk about it over this week?" asked the therapist.

"I suddenly have an idea of what you might be thinking," the wife said. "I don't know. I could be wrong."

"What's your idea?" the therapist asked.

"I'm not going to tell you," she said.

"I'd be curious to hear."

"I'll let you know if I'm right."

"Well, tell me anyway."

"No."

"I'd like to hear it now."

At this point the therapist had been hooked by the wife in exactly the same way he had been dealing with the couple. She was withholding, and he was trying to find out what her idea was. Actually, the therapist could only lose. If she had guessed wrong, it wouldn't matter. If she had correctly guessed what the guaranteed plan was, and she revealed it, she would puncture the whole procedure and it would be ineffective. The therapist needed to drop the issue and go on, but he couldn't.

"I could be way out in left field," the wife said. "So I'll just keep it to myself. My own personal, private little thought."

"It would be important for me to hear it, if you could share it," said the therapist.

"Why? *You* won't tell *me*," she said.

"I'll tell you when I have an agreement with you," the therapist said, looking at them sternly. "I'll tell you, you bet I'll tell you. But you're both going to have to be committed to doing it." He paused and smiled, "But I would like to hear your idea."

"I'm not going to tell you," said the woman, laughing. "It's just an idea. It could be way out in left field."

"If it's way out, we'll just forget it. But if you've hit on the idea, on the method, that would tell me something."

At this point the supervisor behind the one-way mirror intervened by calling the therapist on the telephone and suggesting he drop the issue.

"At any rate," the therapist said, hanging up the phone, "the idea I have will work."

"Why are you sure it will work?"

"I'm not going to explain."

"Have you seen it work?" the husband asked.

"It will work," said the therapist, who, as a matter of fact, had not seen it work. "But it's not going to be easy."

After a silence, the wife asked, "Why would it be difficult?"

"You'll know when I tell you. But it's going to take a solemn commitment from each of you to follow through on this."

Gesturing to both wife and husband, he said, "From you and from you."

When the therapist was sufficiently sure that the couple were committed to doing what he asked, he told them what he wanted them to do. The cure was simple. It had the characteristics necessary for a cure: It was an easily understood directive, it was of such a nature that it would prevent any relapses, it was something the couple could do, and it was an ordeal that was worse than the symptom. In fact, following the directive made the symptom impossible, so that it would simply disappear.

One of the merits of this cure is that it can be used when the therapist doesn't know the purpose or function of a symptom and can't even make up a sufficiently plausible hypothesis. The same task worked with a couple in which the wife had the special problem of compulsive vomiting. Even after several interviews, the therapist could not discover a sufficient reason that she had the problem. Compulsive vomiting is a quite common symptom today in this age of eating disorders, while compulsive washing is from the age of a concern about cleanliness.

This wife had vomited since she was eighteen years old, and so at age thirty-one she had over ten years of practice. Her routine was to binge on junk foods and then vomit them up many times a day. Like the handwasher, she had received a variety of kinds of therapy for the problem with no effect. Unlike the handwasher, she had a more severe problem that could possibly develop if her symptom stopped. She had been diagnosed as a case of anorexia nervosa and had twice been hospitalized for starving herself. If the therapist stopped her from vomiting, she might begin to gain weight, and at that point she could choose self-starvation and end up in the hospital as before.

The therapist, Robert Kirkhorn, asked the husband to come in with the wife. He treated the problem as a couple problem rather than using the individual focus of previous therapists. She was a slim, pretty woman, and her husband was a handsome, pleasant young man. One of the reasons for including the husband in the therapy was the particular nature of this problem. Women who have the vomiting problem do not usually tell the truth about it. It is a secret sin, and the therapist must work with a client who is deceitful about the symptom and also is a procrastinator who does not follow directives well. Including the husband will increase the chances that directives will be followed and will make possible a more truthful reporting of the frequency of vomiting. To include the husband in an ordeal helps prevent the wife from relapsing because it would be a couple relapse, not merely a personal relapse of hers.

This problem seemed so difficult that it was decided to define the first interview as a consultation, not as a first therapy session with a contract to cure. Not only is this type of problem typically a difficult and exasperating one, but this instance was extreme, since the wife was vomiting from four to twenty-five times a day, had done so for over ten years, and had even vomited when in the hospital on a weight gain program for anorexia.

When Mr. Kirkhorn met with the couple, they described her past therapy and her preoccupation with her body. He asked her to describe a typical binge and vomiting session so he could determine how he might intervene to stop the woman from her dedicated bodily self-punishment. "I would like a typical situation around a binging meal," he said. "I would like such details as what you think about beforehand, what your plan is, how you go about executing your plan, where you go when you do it, and so on. Pick a day and describe it."

"All right," the wife said. "When I got up in the morning yesterday, I thought—as I think every day—today I'm going to do well, which means no binging. I plan what I'm going to do for lunch. I think about that all morning long. I also think up tricks, like only taking a certain amount of money. So yesterday, since I didn't want to come to therapy and knew I had to stop this myself, I was determined not to binge. I took a certain amount of money for my lunch, and I took the newspaper to go back and read during my lunch hour. At lunchtime I went to the drugstore and I got a little cup of cabbage and a little cup of coleslaw. That was my lunch. I brought them back to my desk, and I ate them. Then somebody said, 'You want to go out to lunch?' So I said, 'Well, I think so,' because in my mind I was thinking, that's all right, I always have tomorrow. So I went to lunch, and . . ." The wife paused, looking guiltily at her husband, and said, "I bought a cheeseburger, french fries, onion rings, and a bowl of chili. When it was time to go, I bought two cheeseburgers and a grilled cheese sandwich and two french fries to take them back to the office with me. On the way I stopped at the store and I bought four candy bars, a Twinkie cupcake, a doughnut, and a diet Pepsi. I went back to my desk and ate it all. My stomach was out to here," she said, showing a roundness. "Then I went and threw that up."

"How do you make yourself throw up?" the therapist asked.

"I just lean over," she said.

"Do you throw up one time, or several times?"

"You mean is there just one massive outpouring, or is there more than one? There's more than one. I do it continually until I feel it's pretty much all gone. It's several repeated ones. I usually stop for a couple of minutes because in my mind that's giving whatever is in there a chance to get down to where I can bring it up. Usually I keep going until there's nothing but air in there. Then I figure there's got to be a little bit more in there, and so I stop for a few minutes." She turned to her husband. "This is really gross. I'm sorry." The woman's honesty when doing the unfeminine task of frankly describing her gross symptom to two men was evidence to therapist and supervisor that her prognosis was good and therapy might be successful.

"I've heard it before," he said.

The therapist asked the husband, "Have you seen her vomit?"

"No," he said. "Well, I've walked in accidentally and caught her a few times."

"How do you know when you're done?" the therapist asked the woman.

"Sometimes it's just a guess. Sometimes it's because I know what the heaviest thing I've eaten was. For example, I know, when I've had a marshmallow, that it floats. So when the marshmallow comes up, I know I'm pretty close to the end. Or if I had a salad before dinner, when I see the lettuce come up, I figure I'm pretty close to the end because lettuce floats."

"When you vomit, do you find pleasure?" the therapist asked. "Is it enjoyable?"

"No."

"Is any part of it enjoyable?"

"The eating."

"Is any part of the vomiting enjoyable?"

"No, when it's done, it's just a relief."

How severe the problem was became evident in a later interview. Discussing how he had vaguely threatened to leave her, the husband reported, "I've said, 'Someplace down the road I'm going to walk out on you if you don't stop this.' " He said that the threat had been put most severely when the plumbing backed up in their house. "We literally had a basement full of vomit. I mean literally. It backed up three inches deep on the floor of the basement. That was really disgusting."

"Who cleaned it up?" asked the therapist.

"I did," said the husband, while the wife protested that she had once cleaned it up too. "I thought it was a matter of garbage and accumulated debris," said the husband. "I didn't realize what it was until she confessed a week later that it had to be vomit."

A problem with this woman was her history of being hospitalized because she could rapidly lose weight to the point that her life was in danger. The therapist was therefore concerned that she might give up vomiting and respond by not eating. Solving one problem could produce another. An additional possibility was that she might be stopped from vomiting, but if she began to gain weight, she would start to vomit again and so relapse. Accordingly, the therapist was as focused on the weight issue as on the vomiting. He asked how much she weighed, and she said it was ninety-seven pounds.

"What is the most that you have weighed?" he asked.

"A hundred and fifty pounds," she said with disgust, adding that that had been when she was in her teens.

"Tell me," the therapist said, "if you were to think of a weight you could go up to before you would think you would have to begin to vomit again, what weight would that be?" He added, "I would think two hundred pounds would be too much."

The woman looked thoughtful. "Would you like me to be honest? I would say one hundred pounds. At one hundred I start to get nervous."

"What would you consider a normal weight for a woman your size?"

"Another person? A hundred."

"A hundred is when you think you look the best?"

"Sure, because I don't weigh a hundred pounds. If I weighed a hundred, I would probably say ninety-five pounds."

When asked, the husband said he thought that at one hundred and ten or one hundred and fifteen pounds "she looks best and physically is more capable of handling herself."

"I've never weighed one hundred and ten since you've known me," said the wife.

"Well, we set a goal of a weight of a hundred and five," he said, and she agreed they had done that, saying she had weighed that when they first met.

The wife, like most women with eating disorders, was constantly concerned about her weight and typically weighed herself several times a day. At the third interview, the therapist asked the husband to weigh her for one week in a special way. "Weigh her on a daily basis," he said. "Keep a chart of her weight daily. But I'd like you not to let her know what the weight is. Conceal what you read on the scale with your hand, and don't let her see it." To the wife he said, "I don't want you to weigh yourself anywhere for one week."

The goal was to have the wife not focus on her weight for one week to see whether she could tolerate going that long without knowing what she weighed. She not only managed to avoid weighing herself for a week, but from that time on she stopped weighing herself more than once a week. The constant preoccupation with weight disappeared, which was a positive sign that she was giving up her focus on her body.

The therapist asked the husband to keep a log of how many times each day the wife vomited. The husband laughed, saying, "You're expecting her to tell me?"

"I'm assuming you will have that information," said the therapist.

Laughing, the wife said, "You expect me to tell him."

As a matter of fact, she did tell him. The husband kept a daily log and brought it in the following week. The wife's honesty about the vomiting made a cure possible.

Conversation with the couple did not reveal a problem between them or with their families, who lived at a distance, that seemed sufficient to provoke the extreme vomiting that was characteristic of the wife. No reasonable hypothesis for the vomiting could be proposed. In such a case, a therapist is often concerned about what to do and also about tampering with someone's life without knowing what might be the function of a severe symptom. To deal with this problem, the therapist asked the couple to make a list, spending some time together each night, of all the consequences they could think of that could occur should the wife stop vomiting. The emphasis was not on negative consequences of the vomiting, such as risking the loss of her teeth, as vomiters do when acids from the stomach regularly come into the mouth, or damage to the esophagus. They were to discuss such issues as what she would do with all that time that she was now using to vomit. There would also be the change in their relationship if she was no longer the helpless "problem person" but had made such an extraordinary change as giving up a ten-year symptom, and so on.

The husband and wife came in the following week with the list typed neatly in triplicate—two pages, single-spaced, of all the consequences they could think of. The next two sessions were devoted to going over the list of consequences. The attitude of the therapist was that he could solve this problem, but he wasn't sure he should do so until he knew what the consequences were. The husband and wife emphasized that she wouldn't have to be dishonest and he'd be able to trust her. They would have to adapt to a more trusting, intimate relationship. If she recovered and solved her difficult problem, they would also have to experience a new marriage contract, since the husband had married a woman with a problem she could not solve. If she solved the problem, she would no longer be the problem in the relationship.

To test out their willingness to follow instructions, the couple were given various tasks. The husband was asked to go with the wife and shop for a complete lunch of junk food for a proper binge, and then she was to eat it in front of him and go vomit. Each task given to them was carried out by this cooperative couple. Finally it was decided they were appropriate for an ordeal. Since they were cooperative with minor tasks, they were likely to carry out a major one. It was decided to set up the ordeal as a guaranteed cure. In the sixth interview, the therapist began the shaggy-dog technique. He said, "There are two things I'm going to ask you to do. One is going to seem pretty minor. The second one will, in fact, solve the problem." The therapist then said he would see them in two weeks, when the solution to the problem would be given to them. Before that he wanted them to do a minor task. He outlined the task, which was to shop once again for the binge lunch and bring it all home. The husband and wife were to sit and look at the food together, and the wife was to decide whether to eat it or throw it out. "You will have a choice of two ways to throw away the food," said the therapist. "One way is through your body, the other is through the garbage disposal or the toilet."

One purpose of this task was to allow the couple an opportunity to voluntarily give up the problem. If the wife decided not to eat the lunch but to throw it away, then she was making a decision to give up the vomiting. As a matter of fact, they reported later that she cheerfully ate the food while talking about the decision whether to eat it.

When the therapist said he could solve the problem, the husband looked worried, saying, "That gives me a twinge in the stomach," and tears came to the wife's eyes. The therapist began a long discourse about this and that, leaving the couple more and more frustrated about learning his solution for their problem. Discussing the task, the therapist said, "What I will ask you to do now is laying the foundation for resolving this problem. The foundation is important in that it really lets me know whether you two are serious or not. What that foundation is, without going into what the resolution of the problem will be, is that starting today, for the next two weeks, you must be completely, totally, without fail, honest in telling your husband each day about times you vomit. The issue of honesty must be completely agreed upon beforehand. Can you be completely, totally, sincerely, wholeheartedly honest?"

"Yes," said the wife, adding, "but how will you know that I am?"

"I won't know," the therapist said, "and that's why I'm asking you to be totally, completely honest during these next two weeks."

"I can promise."

To the husband, the therapist said, "It's important that you be kind. If she says a large number of times when she reports to you about the vomiting, you shouldn't let your eyes bug out or have your pen go through the paper in shock. You have to be gentle with her and not judgmental."

"I will," he said, and immediately the wife added that she would be certain to be honest.

The therapist said, "The important thing to realize is this: I don't want either of you to do this unless you're absolutely, totally committed to getting over this problem. I will guarantee a solution if you do what I say, but if you're not ready for a solution, I don't want to do this."

"I promise," said the wife. "But it's a little frightening. I can't believe I get something out of doing it, but I must get something out of it. I just don't know." When the therapist said again that she didn't have to get over the problem, she said, "I want to do it. I've followed your instructions exactly before, and I can do it again. I'll do it."

In two weeks the couple came in with a chart of the number of vomits. They were willing to do whatever they were told. At that point, they would have done just about any task the therapist could have proposed. The careful preparation during seven interviews was done to motivate them to do whatever would be harder on them than the symptom. Committing both husband and wife to the task made it more difficult for them to back out of any agreement, as they might if only one person had been committed.

Rather than tell them the task immediately, the therapist began to chat with them about other things. He admired the chart, he asked about work, and generally he chatted for most of the hour. Discussing the chart, he protested that the highest day had been only seven vomits, which wasn't all that many. He also asked them whether they wanted to discuss with each other for a while whether they were really committed to getting over

the problem, and they said they did not. They had discussed
that *ad nauseam* and were ready to get over it.

Finally the therapist said, "It will be important that we
meet again next Thursday."

They agreed to that.

"We need to meet at six o'clock. Is that agreeable?"

They agreed to that.

"All right, this is what I want you to do, starting today."
He paused. "The next time you vomit, I want you to give me a
penny. I will do with that penny what I see fit."

The couple looked at each other, rather puzzled, and
said, "Okay."

"Is that agreed upon?" asked the therapist. "One penny
from both of you."

The couple nodded in agreement.

"The second time you vomit," said the therapist, "I want
the two of you to give me *two* pennies. Again, I will use them as
I see fit. This money will be independent of your normal fee for
coming to the institute. The third time that you vomit, you will
give me *four* pennies. And I want cash. I'm not interested in a
check. I want the cash to be brought here next week. The
fourth time that you vomit, you're going to bring me *eight*
cents. Again, that is money to use as I see fit. You two will not
have any decision in what I decide to do with that money."

The couple stared at the therapist, still puzzled.

"Now let us get a definition of terms," said the therapist.
"A vomit is anything that comes out of your stomach, be it
forced or controlled or uncontrolled. You might get the flu and
vomit. That counts."

"Okay," the wife said.

The therapist reviewed the sequence again, from one to
two to four to eight, and so on. "It will continue at that rate,
and you will bring me all that money in cash next Thursday at
six o'clock."

"It doubles, doubles, doubles," said the husband.

"That's right," said the therapist. (At the following interview he added that the contract continued until the woman was
eighty years old.)

The wife looked upset, the husband puzzled; the therapist dismissed them.

When they came in the following week, husband and wife said they hadn't understood how this was actually a guaranteed cure. When they sat down with paper and pencil to calculate the cost of future vomiting, they discovered that by the twentieth vomit the doubling would increase the cost of each vomit to thousands of dollars. She had to stop vomiting or they would go bankrupt. They brought in $1.28 for eight vomits she had done, but then the therapist discovered that one of the vomits had been prior to the interview the previous week and they had counted it because it had occurred that day. He reduced the charge to 64 cents, making a bureaucratic issue of being exact.

The following week the wife had vomited only once more, and so the charge was again up to $1.28. When the therapist suggested the possibility of a relapse, the wife said she hadn't thought of it, but now that he had mentioned it, she might have one. He said he would look forward to it, implying that there would be a financial benefit to himself. He said there were things he would like to buy, and the wife replied, "Me too." She did not relapse. The couple were seen over the next few months, reviewing the consequences of giving up the symptom as they had previously outlined them, and the wife went through considerable change, as did the husband. She became more assertive, changed to a better job, and developed considerably more self-confidence, as usually happens when someone recovers from a severe symptom. The husband improved in a similar way.

The choice of using pennies was the result of collaboration between therapist and supervisor. The supervisor was worried about using dollars because if the wife took too long to stop her vomiting, it would be too expensive. The therapist suggested using pennies, which was exactly correct for this couple.

Now, the handwashing couple had been dealt with in terms of dollars. If the wife washed her hands abnormally, it was one dollar each time the first week. The second week, it was two dollars for each abnormal washing. The third week, it was three dollars each time, and so on. If the husband reassured the wife about the handwashing, he had to pay a dollar and then two dollars, and so on.

When the couple came in two weeks after the instruction, the husband had not reassured his wife once and so did not owe a dollar. The wife had done ten abnormal handwashings the first week and one the second.

Accepting the money, the therapist said, "Only once the second week?"

"Sorry about that," the wife said, laughing.

When asked whether she was sure these were the only "abnormal" washings, she said they were, but she added, "Am I allowed to stretch a point or not?," meaning that at times she was uncertain whether she was washing abnormally or just normally washing her hands.

"If you can do it in good conscience, that's up to you," said the therapist.

The wife agreed to make the distinction, forcing herself to be honest, and she continued to be so. The therapist offered them the rationale for giving it up that the less she did it, the more the desire to do it would be extinguished.

"I can believe that," said the woman. "I've seen that. I even used a public toilet this week."

"Did you?"

"I thought I'd have a nervous breakdown afterwards. I had to go to the bathroom when I went to look at those houses for sale. I thought, now, should I wait three hours or should I go?" She laughed. "So I went because I thought, you know, the damage from waiting would probably be worse than going."

Turning to the husband, the therapist said, "It's all right with you if your wife uses a public bathroom?"

"Oh, yeah, I think that's what they are there for," said the husband.

"For just anybody?"

"Probably."

"I was a wreck afterwards, because I wasn't allowed to wash my hands fourteen times to make sure that I had washed them once. And that was terrible."

"But it's very good you were able to do it."

"Well," said the husband, "it's just like a habit is what it is, right?"

"Ask Sarah," said the therapist. "You know, I'm only an expert, and Sarah has stumped the experts many times."

The couple were seen for several more interviews, and the act of washing as well as the desire disappeared. A follow-up showed that the problem was over.

In these two cases, the solution was simple, and yet it met the proper criteria of an ordeal. It was a task that was worse than the symptom, and it was something the couples could do. By committing both husband and wife to the task, the therapist increased the odds that there would be no backing out. In both cases the relationship with the therapist was such that they were fond of him but did not really want to enrich him at their expense.

Where would such an absurd solution come from? Looking back, there are two possible origins in the work of Milton H. Erickson. When faced with intractable pain that had no physical cause, such as severe headaches that occurred twenty-four hours a day, Erickson would suggest to a patient in hypnosis that sometime during the next day the person would have one second without pain. A patient would concede that that might happen. Erickson would help make it seem reasonable by saying that perhaps the person might slip while going down the steps and for that moment he would be distracted and not have pain. Or at the moment he was going to the bathroom he might be without pain for one second. After the possibility of one second without pain was established, Erickson would say that there could even be two seconds without pain. After discussing this awhile, he would say that in a busy day or during sleep at night there could even be four seconds or as much as eight seconds without pain. Earlier in the interview, Erickson would have talked casually with the person about geometric progression—about how numbers can double from one to two to four to eight, and so on. The patient would agree that once that progression started, the numbers kept doubling, because it is in the nature of that progression that the numbers double in that way. When the time came that the person in hypnosis conceded that he might be without pain one second, and then two, and then four, and so on, he was accepting the geometric progression that ultimately led to being without pain.

The possibility of using geometric progression came from that idea. The possibility of using money as a way of stopping a symptom also came from an idea by Erickson. A man once came to him asking him to cure his son of a problem of not being able to urinate in a public bathroom if anyone else was present. The son had had this problem all his life and in college had mapped out the bathrooms so that he could always be alone. He was to enter the Navy in thirty days. On a ship that kind of privacy would be impossible. So the man asked Erickson to cure the son. The father was a difficult man who was an alcoholic and was mean, as Erickson found out from the man's wife. He was also rude and insulting to Erickson, even though he was asking Erickson to cure his son. So Erickson told the man that he would cure the son on one condition: The father would have to post a bond of $3,000, which was to go to Erickson to use as he saw fit if the father took one drink. Erickson could give back the money, keep it and vacation, or do what he pleased with it. After soul searching, the father agreed because he wished to have his son cured.

Erickson cured the son within the thirty days, and the father did not take another drink. The mother reported to Erickson that the old man had even become a reasonable person since he had stopped drinking. At Christmas the man called Erickson and said, "I would like to have one beer, but I don't wish it to cost me $3,000. Can we arrange that I have one beer?"

"How big a beer?" asked Erickson.

"I thought you'd ask that," said the man.

They agreed on an eight-ounce glass of beer, and Erickson generously allowed him to have one on both Christmas and New Year's Day.

3

———◆——◆——◆——◆——◆——◆——◆——◆——◆———

Your Mother's Moustache

The therapist, Dr. Wimalapathy Ismail, was in her last year of training as a psychiatric resident at Howard University. A large woman who wore a colorful sari, she was from Ceylon and had six grown children. One day she was interviewing a thin, depressed woman, Ms. Simpkins, who had recently stopped working and asked for therapy. Ms. Simpkins lacked interest in work and everything else. Dr. Ismail sat quietly listening to the slim, attractive young black woman while a supervisor observed from behind a one-way mirror. The woman said she had given up a good job as an executive secretary and was sitting at home living on unemployment insurance. She had no interest in working or in social life. For several years she had had a boyfriend who drove a taxi. He made little money, since he only occasionally drove the taxi. The implication was that Ms. Simpkins had been supporting the boyfriend with her good salary. When asked what else she had been supporting, she mentioned a large house on which she made the payments. Years before her father had disappeared. Her mother had died nine years previously, leaving her the house and the mortgage payments. Only when pressed did Ms. Simpkins bring up the fact that she was also supporting her brother. She brought him up as an afterthought. He was twenty-nine years old and sat in the living room, almost never going out. As a young man he had gone to college for a period, but he had stopped that and begun a life of sitting and doing nothing. Not only was Ms. Simpkins supporting him and putting a roof over his head, but she cooked the meals, she did the shopping, and she cleaned the house around him. Her brother spoke little and only when spoken to. She said he was honest, always a man of his word, and he was pleasant, but he just did not do anything.

Dr. Ismail focused the woman on the issue of her boyfriend. He declined to come to the therapy interviews. As the woman talked about him over several sessions, he disappeared from her life, apparently because she was no longer working and supporting him. Ms. Simpkins cheered up somewhat as the boyfriend disappeared, and the therapist began to suspect that the woman might have quit her job because she was tired of such burdens. Perhaps even more improvement might occur if Ms. Simpkins could cease supporting the brother who only sat in the living room. The therapist asked her to bring the brother to the next session.

When the woman and the brother arrived, he proved to be a nice-looking man dressed in working clothes. His name was Oscar, and he would say nothing voluntarily; when asked a question, he answered politely. The most striking feature about Oscar was his moustache. He had a large, bushlike moustache, which hid the lower part of his face. The moustache was impressive and carefully trimmed. Obviously the man took care of it. Except for the moustache, everything about him was a monotone. He wore a bored, bland expression, spoke in a monotonous voice, and hardly moved to gesture. His clothes were worn and nondescript.

The therapist explained to Oscar that she had asked him

to come in because his sister was unhappy and needed assistance to get her life organized and to feel like living again. When asked whether she had once been cheerful and capable, Oscar said that she had. When asked whether she had changed and now seemed to be uninterested in living, he said that was true. The therapist asked him whether he was willing to help his sister. After a long pause, he said there was nothing he could do.

Ms. Simpkins, with a gesture of despair, said that her brother always said he could do nothing. She said those pants were his only pants; that shirt was his only shirt. When they needed washing, he sat in his underwear while she washed them, and then he put them back on. His shoes had an unused look because in the house he went barefoot, and he never went out of the house.

"How long since you have been out of the house?" asked the therapist.

Oscar looked thoughtful and finally said, "Quite a while."

The therapist asked Oscar about his mother's death, and he said it had been a long time ago. The sister said it had happened nine years previously, and she proceeded to tell a remarkable story. Apparently Oscar had been his mother's pride and joy. He had done well in high school and had entered college intending to be a lawyer. He studied hard in college and held a job on the side to pay his expenses. He also had an active social life. Hoping to go to the best law school, he got excellent grades. His mother and sister were proud of him. It hurt Oscar to see how hard his mother worked on her hands and knees to support him and his sister. He loved his mother and was determined to succeed and keep his mother in comfort for the rest of her life.

His mother became ill and suddenly died. After the funeral, Oscar and his sister came home to the house. Oscar sat down in the living room and stared in front of him. The next day he didn't go to classes. His sister and his friends thought that it was a temporary distress from the sudden shock, that he'd soon recover from mourning his mother and go back to his regular life. He didn't. He sat in the house and didn't go out. His friends urged him to get back to school, but he said he did not wish to go. After a while his friends abandoned him and went about their business. His sister encouraged him, and when he didn't move, she became angry and fought with him. She said he had to get out and work to support himself. He didn't move. She tried everything she could think of to move him. At one point she took him to a psychiatrist for regular visits. He talked about his mother in a matter-of-fact way and said he would rather not do anything. Exasperated with paying for his therapy when he didn't improve, and tired of taking him there regularly, the sister stopped taking him. Oscar stopped seeing the psychiatrist.

Ms. Simpkins had been working and supporting her brother all those years, not knowing quite what else to do. He did a little cleaning around the house, but essentially he did nothing but sit, as if lost in thought. He was polite about everything and did not act crazy in any way. He simply would not take any action.

Ms. Simpkins said sadly, "Now I'm out of work after nine years, and we can hardly eat or afford the mortgage. Still he does nothing. We're going to lose the house."

"What if you lose the house?" the therapist asked Oscar.

"That would be too bad," he said.

The sister said the city would take him and put him in an institution if he had no place to live. Oscar agreed that would probably happen.

"I would like you to help your sister," said the therapist.

"I'd like to myself, but I can't," said Oscar.

As they talked, the sister became more depressed. It seemed quite clear to therapist and supervisor that a part of her lack of interest in living was due to this man sitting at home wasting what had been a promising life.

The therapist interviewed Oscar alone and talked with him about his mother. He said he had loved her, but her death had not been so terrible a blow. He had missed her, but only as any son would miss a mother. He just could not do anything. He said that probably if he ever started doing something, he would go on doing it, but he could not start anything. He agreed that he'd probably starve or be institutionalized if his sister didn't support him, but there was nothing he could do about it. He also agreed that his being a burden was probably related to his sister's disinterest in living. His eyes were sad above his large moustache as he said that it was an unfortunate situation.

After making a plan, the therapist interviewed Oscar and his sister together. She asked Ms. Simpkins whether she would be willing to go and get a job if her brother went to work. Ms. Simpkins said her brother would never go to work. When pressed, she said that if he did do the unbelievable and got a job, she would get her old job back or get a new job and begin to take an interest in life again. But she said that her brother would never go out and get a job.

The therapist pointed out to Oscar that his sister seemed to have withdrawn from the working world and lost interest in life when she found herself burdened by supporting a boyfriend who did not want to take responsibility and get married. She also had lost interest in life because all she gained from working so hard was to support a perfectly healthy brother who sat and did nothing. Now that the boyfriend was out of the picture, the next step would be for Oscar to go to work. His sister would come out of her indifferent state and begin to live again when she knew he was doing all right and supporting himself.

"I'm sure that's all true," said Oscar agreeably, "but there is nothing I can do." He looked at his sister, his eyes large behind the huge moustache.

Finally the therapist said to Oscar, "You have not been able to get to work, but I can get you to go to work. I can guarantee that you will go out and get a job. But you must agree to do what I say if you don't get a job."

He stared at her, puzzled. She continued, "I want you to agree that on next Monday—which is one week from today—you will have a job and be working, or you will do what I say."

"Do what?" he asked.

"Something that will make you go to work because you won't want to do it. Yet it will be something you can easily do. It will only take a few minutes and be no trouble. Yet you will go to work rather than do it."

"Nothing will make him go to work," said the sister.

"This will," said the therapist.

"It doesn't sound like it," said the sister. "If it's something that only takes a few minutes, it's not enough to make him go to work."

"I guarantee it," said the therapist, solemnly adjusting her sari, as if giving what she said the authority of the ancient East.

"I must agree without knowing what it is?" asked Oscar, one of the few occasions when he volunteered a statement. He looked amused, and there seemed to be more life to him as his curiosity was aroused.

"You must agree to do it if you are not working on Monday," said the therapist. "I will talk to you alone to tell you what it is, but first you must agree to do it. I'm sure you can get a job with your educational background."

"Of course he could," said Ms. Simpkins. "I have friends who would hire him."

After some discussion, the sister was asked to leave the room. Alone with Oscar, the therapist said, "Are you willing?"

"Willing to do what?" he asked.

"Willing to do what I say if you are not working next Monday." She smiled, "You say you can do nothing, but you can say yes to me. And I know that if you agree, you will keep your word, because you are an honest man."

"That is why I do not wish to agree lightly," he said. "You might ask me to do something terrible."

"Nothing more terrible than wasting your life as you are doing now," said the therapist.

"I would rather know what it is before I agree," said Oscar.

"No," said the therapist, "you must agree without knowing what it is. And you will never know what it is if you don't agree to do it."

Oscar was thoughtful for a long time, long enough for the therapist to wonder whether he had forgotten she was there. Then he seemed to go through some inner turmoil. Finally he said, "All right, I'll agree to do what you say if I'm not working next Monday. What must I do?"

"You must shave off your moustache," said Dr. Ismail.

Oscar looked at her, stunned. He put his hand to the one possession of which he was proud.

She said, "This agreement is between you and me and not to be told to your sister." Standing, she gestured Oscar out the door.

When the sister came in for an interview two days later, she said with astonishment that her brother had been out looking for a job every day. That morning he had an interview where they might very well hire him. She asked the therapist what she had said to him that had transformed him. The therapist did not tell her. Instead, she pointed out that Ms. Simpkins herself had agreed to go back to work and to get her life together if her brother got a job.

The next Monday, the brother was working, but he would not come in again to see the therapist. The sister also went to work. She continued with the therapist for two months and became interested in life again. She reported that her brother seemed to have recovered from his mother's death. He had become self-supporting and was seeing friends again.

4

~~~~~~~~~~~~~~~~~~~~~~~~~~~~~~~~~~~~

A Child Who
Falls Out

The problem could be heard two blocks away because the three-year-old boy yelled whenever his family took him outside the house. He also yelled inside the house if he was told to do anything or not to do something. Often he threw himself on the floor and banged on it with his fists while yelling. Seeming to imitate this erupting volcano, his two-year-old sister also regularly threw herself to the floor and screamed. The children might have stepped out of the nightmares of a couple who feared having children.

The mother and father were working-class people who had dressed the children with special care for the visit. The boy was in a suit and tie, and the girl wore a ruffled white dress and white shoes. Large and plump, the mother wore a brown wig and looked harassed as she struggled with the children and two bags full of diapers and bottles. The father, dressed in a suit, was small and slim.

When the family came for the interview, the boy made everyone aware of his arrival by yelling all the way to the therapy room. He appeared to be almost unmanageable unless physically restrained. He was also famous in his neighborhood and at the clinics and hospitals his mother visited. Professionals were always advising her what to do about his yelling. The advice had not proved helpful.

When Janice White, the therapist, brought the family into the interview room, the boy immediately ran and grabbed a telephone on a desk. The mother said, "Don't touch that telephone!" The father said, "Leave that phone alone!" The boy began to yell, as he usually did when told not to do something. Throughout the interview the children ran about and often screamed, making it difficult for the therapist and parents to hear one another. The parents could not be interviewed without the children because, when separated from his parents, the boy screamed in panic.

The therapist asked the father what problem had brought him there. The father hesitated and seemed to minimize the situation. He didn't like to describe their difficulties with the boy because he was in disagreement with his wife about whether there was really a problem about which something should be done. He said, "I don't know, I just think he's a little bit spoiled. Before the baby came, he was all right. He didn't have any problems. All he used to do was holler a lot. Now he just falls out. Like if she's [the daughter's] got something that's hers, he going to take it away from her. Another thing, you tell him to sit down, he'll fall down on the floor. She done picked up the habit from him."

The mother had a notebook in her hand to remind herself of the points she wished to make. When asked about the problem, she presented it as a more serious one. While talking to the therapist, she was constantly distracted by something the children were doing and was often getting up and down to deal with them, putting her wig in disarray. She said she had been helpless to solve the problem despite her efforts to do what the experts said. When asked what she had come to the clinic for, she said, "This child was about eight months old when I was pregnant with her [the daughter]. They told me when I have this baby here, that when I came home from the hospital to treat both of them alike. So I mean, he was already—like I was trying to toilet-train him. After the baby came, he didn't want to sit on the potty anymore. I tried to get him away from the bottle, but he still wanted to take the bottle. Well, I took him back to a clinic . . ." Interrupted by the boy's getting in a desk drawer, she brought him by the hand back to her chair. As she sat him down and continued talking, the father told the boy to sit in a different chair. The boy yelled, and the mother continued talking over the noise. "So when I took him back, I said he still wants to act like a baby. So the lady told me, she said, 'Well, he's around the other child, keep the diapers on him, let him take the bottle, and gradually kind of wean him away from it.' So that's what I've been trying to do. That's the problem. He's partially pot-trained, and he's using the pot very good for to urinate in, but he won't have a bowel movement in it. He still messes on himself. When something doesn't go right, then he starts screaming and hollering and throwing things. Then, like if I take him outside, people from two blocks around can tell when he comes outside because he hollers so much."

Asked how she got the boy to stop a tantrum, the mother said, "I tell him, I yell at him, I say, 'Stop!,' you know. But sometimes it does good and sometimes it doesn't. Sometimes I have to spank him. Like he has the habit now that when I tell him something, he spits. And I told him, I said, 'Arnold, that's very nasty, don't do that.' " She added that sometimes she slapped him in the mouth when he didn't stop spitting.

The description by mother and father was often interrupted by the children's being noisy and obstreperous and so illustrating what they said. The therapist managed to talk above the noise while also observing the parents dealing with their children. Observers and supervisor behind the one-way mirror also had the opportunity to observe the family. Although the mother talked about spanking the boy and slapping his mouth, it appeared that this kind of abuse occurred rarely. The parents did not seem to be abusing parents in the sense that some action needed to be taken for the children's sake.

As the parents talked, the disagreement between them became quite evident. The father put it as a competitive issue. He said, "But see, he obey me a whole lot more now than he do his mother. I don't have no problem, like when I'm home the weekend, I don't have a problem. I don't—they don't cry. They don't holler. They sit down and play. When it's time for their nap, they go to bed at twelve o'clock. Sometimes it's one o'clock or one-thirty." As the father said this, the mother was dragging each of the children back to her chair, and they were both yelling. As the mother sat the boy down, the father called him to come to sit by *him,* contradicting mother's instruction.

When asked whether she thought the children obeyed the father better, the mother agreed. She had been told it was because the father's voice was deeper. Actually, observing the parents with the children, they didn't seem to obey the father more than the mother (nor did his voice seem to be deeper than hers).

Particularly defensive about her childrearing ability, the mother commented on how she had tried to do what the experts said and nothing had helped. As an example, she talked about what the people at the hospital had told her to do when Arnold "falls out like that." "They told me to ignore him," she said. "There's only but so much you can ignore, you understand what I mean? I mean, you take the child out, you got two of them, they're nothing but babies. And I mean, you try to keep one quiet, and the other one she's falling out. Then sometimes both of them is falling out together. And I mean it's hard on me, you know what I mean? Like I mean it makes you feel bad when you take children out and they holler like that."

The mother described a trip to the store, saying, "In the store, like they—every day I take them out, and we go in the store, and he starts screaming before I can even get in the door. Then *she* starts to act up. And the lady tells me, 'If they holler, don't bring them in here.' What was I supposed to do?" Interrupted by the children quarreling, she shouted at them to stop the noise. "And the doctor told me to—when he does that, just go in another room . . ." She shrugged helplessly.

Typically, when children have problems, the parents are

in disagreement about some aspect of the problem. In this family, father and mother disagreed about whether there was a problem at all. As part of the routine of a first interview, the therapist asked them to discuss the problem, and the mother said, "George, do you think Arnold has a problem?"

"No," replied the father.

"I do," said the mother. "I think he does."

"If you think he does, then have him checked out. I don't think there's nothing wrong with him. Just like I told you —I told you a couple of months ago. You got to give him a chance."

The mother said she wanted to give him a chance, but after a while they'd want to put the boy in nursery school. "These problems he's having now with this falling out and all this hollering, those people is not gonna put up with that. Am I right?"

"You don't know if he's gonna have them," said the father. "You have to give the child a chance." When the mother said she wanted to give him a chance, he replied, "Not if you think something's wrong with him. I don't think no child can be treated for it. He can't be treated for it, it's just a natural way."

At that moment the boy erupted into yelling and screaming, and the mother said, "There, like that, you tell him to stop, he should stop it."

"Well, he's doing what he can," said the father. "He's just only—he just turned three years old."

"You don't know what you're talking about," said the mother.

"All right, you have your way—and I'll have mine."

"It's not like I have my way, George."

"Well, you just have your way."

On the question whether the child was "normal," the father said, "Well, he's normal, it looks like to me. He just have a little habit of yelling and screaming and hollering."

"It's not normal," said the mother, "for a child his age to just stand up and scream and holler." She turned to the therapist. "Now I'm home with these children all day. These little things, I see them, because I'm home with the children when

he's on the job, you understand what I mean?" She added that
she wanted her child to have a chance "so I can say, 'Well, I
done my part,' you understand what I mean? These are my children—they're the only two I will ever have." (She had had a
hysterectomy.) She began to cry. "I mean it's hard when in a
family situation both the mother and father can't see eye to
eye on one particular thing. All right, then if I see he has a problem, then the father feels he don't have a problem, then what
do we do?"

When the mother said there was something wrong with
the boy, the father responded as if she were saying that he himself had something wrong with him. He talked about the boy
not only as if he didn't have a solvable problem but as if the
boy represented *him*. He implied that the problem was his wife,
not the children.

Although the mother was more clear about whether the
boy had a problem, she was more hopeless than the father
about trying to do something. The variety of advice she had
been given, she had been unable to use. The mother was also
physically unwell. She had been in the hospital six times for a
series of operations and was about to have another one; what
might be done was limited by her physical state.

Ordinarily a therapist might call on relatives for assistance, but the extended kin in this case seemed not to be available. Father's family was in another city, and mother's family
consisted of a mother and grandmother. Mother's mother was
"a playgirl" who would not even babysit while the mother was
in the hospital, and the grandmother was quite old and could
help only occasionally.

The therapist was faced with a problem boy who not
only was wild, yelling, and uncontrollable but seemed to be limited in intelligence and speech and was barely responsive when
the therapist played with him in the interview. He could not be
out of the room away from his mother or father without constant screaming and panic.

In childrearing practices, the parents seemed inconsistent
with the children and either overreacted or underreacted to
their behavior. Neither mother nor father seemed to follow

through on rewards and punishments. Consistently they contradicted each other's discipline as if in competition to prove something about childrearing, and they offered no combined leadership to the wild and distressed children.

When faced with this kind of problem, a therapist would ordinarily assume that it would be necessary to educate the parents in childrearing practices. The parents would be taught by an expert how to deal with children of this age, with an emphasis on being consistent and supporting each other's instructions to the children. There might even be a behavior modification procedure in which the parents applied a reinforcement schedule that would change the children's behavior. The assumption would be that the parents didn't know how to parent or they wouldn't have such problem children.

There are many ways to think about what causes problem children. The history of child therapy has seen a change over the years. First, it was thought that something inside the child was wrong, and therapists did play therapy to change the child's ideas and emotions. When that failed, it began to be noticed that the mother was not dealing with the child correctly, often being inconsistent and helpless, and it was hypothesized that she was causing the child's problem. The mother was put in therapy herself or educated in childrearing practices. Then it began to be noticed that these mothers were often intelligent women who surely knew how to parent effectively. The problem seemed to be what happened if they were competent. When the mother behaved competently, something happened to the father. The father disappeared or became depressed or in some other way was not involved. He became involved only when the mother could not parent effectively. At that point it was hypothesized that it was an organizational problem: Child, mother, and father must be participating in such a way that the problem continued. By the 1960s, all family members were brought together in interviews to change the sequences that led to distress.

The sequence typically followed when there is a child problem can be simplified, ignoring its incredible complexity, to a few steps. The sequence can begin with any starting point, but let us begin with the behavior of the problem child. Typically

the child misbehaves in some way, the mother attempts to deal
with him, and she does so ineffectively. She then complains to
father, and he steps in and is firm with the child, who begins to
behave correctly. The father then withdraws, the child misbehaves again, and mother again deals with him ineffectively. She
complains to father, he intervenes again, and so on. (Of course,
the same situation can occur with a father handling the child ineffectively and the mother stepping in and being firm; the sex of the
parents is not the issue, but their performance in the sequence.
The adults involved can also be other than parents.)

     If we think of the problem as one involving sequences in
a system rather than ignorance about childrearing, the therapy
task is how to change the sequence so everyone behaves differently and so feels differently. In this family with the yelling
children, it was decided to do an experimental therapy that
would carefully avoid all parent education. The assumption behind this strategy was that the parents knew perfectly well how
to parent and that the children were quite capable of normal
behavior. Observation of parents, including quite uneducated
people, had shown they knew how to parent without the advice
of professionals. They raised well-functioning children, seeming
to know that a parent should reward and punish consistently
and adults should support each other when dealing with children. This elementary set of ideas is not complex and is present
everywhere in the culture. Young parents learn to parent from
extended families, from friends, and from popular magazines
and television. If parents are dealing with children in ineffective
ways, it does not follow that the parents are stupid or ignorant.
Nor does it necessarily mean that the parents are driven by unconscious forces programmed from when they were small and
so are raising children the same ways they were raised. It can
simply mean that certain types of organization incapacitate people for functioning normally. The sequences people get caught
up in keep repeating even though the participants would like
things to be different.

     With this family it was decided to try to solve the prob-
lem without in any way teaching mother or father how to deal
with children. There would be no discussion of childrearing

practices, no advice about how to be effective parents, and no "modeling" of how the children should be treated. The therapist would also not do therapy alone with either of the children, and so there would be no form of play therapy. The focus would be on changing the sequences in the family with specific directives, including ordeals. If the children's problems ended, the hypothesis would be supported that parent education is not essential for the therapy of children. Should the parents begin to behave like parents who know how to parent, the hypothesis would be supported that the problem is not an educational one but an organizational one. If that proved to be so, one could wonder about the many years spent educating parents in what they already knew.

The task of the therapist was not simple. She was to change the family without in any way advising the parents about childrearing practices or even talking about childraising. If the mother talked about how to raise children, the therapist would be unresponsive and divert her to other matters. Yet if one does not talk to a mother of a problem child about childrearing, what can one talk about? If two parents are present, they can be encouraged to talk to each other, and so the therapist can avoid offering childrearing advice. However, in this case the father declined to come to the therapy, and so the therapist had only mother to talk with in the first few sessions. The therapist accepted the father's reluctance to come by asking him to come at times if called on. It didn't seem worthwhile to argue with father or drag him in reluctantly if other ways of producing a change could be used.

The plan was to make it as pleasant as possible for mother when she came to the therapy. At the second interview she seemed more at ease, and the children played with toys while the two women talked. The mother seemed less tense and angry when the husband was not present. A variety of ways were used to avoid talking about childrearing. First of all, the mother's physical health was discussed. She expressed her appreciation for the way her husband helped her with the children when she was ill and took care of them when she was hospitalized. She said he did more than most men would.

One of the ways the therapist avoided talking about how to raise children was to ask the mother to talk about what her life would be like *after* the children were over the problem. The mother said she expected to do more with her husband and to go back to work as a practical nurse, which had been her work for nine years. As the mother talked about the future, she occasionally made comments about how to raise children. She said she felt that adults should support each other when dealing with a child who misbehaved. Obviously she had this knowledge without any instruction from the therapist. She talked about how she didn't like her grandmother to interfere when she disciplined the children, and she talked about how she backed up her husband. She reported that once when she had come in, she had asked her husband, "What's wrong with Arnold?" The husband had said he had just spanked him for pushing the baby up against the sideboard. The mother said, "When I came in, Arnold wanted me to pet him. I said, 'No, I'm not going to pet you. When your father corrects you, he knows what he's doing,' and I made him go right over there in the chair and sit down."

Obviously the mother understood the importance of consistency, of adults' supporting each other when raising children, and of behavior control procedures like "time out" in a chair.

In the second interview, the mother was asked not to complain to father when he came home from work. The therapist said, "This week, in the evening when George comes home from work—you usually talk to him about what the kids did?"

"Yeah," said the mother.

"This coming week, when he asks how were the kids today, you say that you handled them okay."

The mother said, "Yeah, every day when he comes in, the first thing he asks me is, how was Arnold today?"

"Well, this time I want you to tell him you handled everything all right. Ask him how *his* day was, talk to him about that."

The mother agreed, summarizing, "Well, you say when he comes and ask me how was Arnold today, I say, 'I handled it.'"

The request that she not complain to her husband was

based on an assumption about the sequences between them. If the sequence is that a mother behaves ineffectively with a child and then the father steps in to deal with him, the father must know that the mother is being ineffective. When he is home, he can observe her as she behaves helplessly. When he is out of the house at work, the mother typically reports to him when he comes home. Often it appears that mother observes father, and if he is depressed, she complains more, which leads him to action with the child that makes him feel better. In this case, the mother was asked not to complain to father about how the children behaved—which would be telling him she was ineffective. She was just to say that she had handled them all right. Their usual sequence could not continue if she followed this instruction. The mother followed the directive, as she followed all those she was given.

If a therapist offers advice to a mother, the mother is accepting the idea that she is incompetent and needs the advice. In this case the therapist avoided offering all advice, implying that the mother was capable of doing without it. In addition, she told the mother that the problem was that she was restraining herself—she should trust her impulses. She was not told what to do with the children, but she was defined as a competent person who would make the correct decisions when free to do so. "Do what *you* feel is best," said the therapist to the mother.

"I'm glad you say that," said the mother.

The therapist added, "From what I see myself, I think your instincts are fine, and you can rely on them. What you'll be doing will be the right thing to do."

During the second interview, the boy knocked a poster from the wall again and again. Mother helplessly protested and patiently put the poster back up time after time. At the next interview, the boy hit the poster once, the mother told him firmly not to do that again, and the boy did not do it again. Had the therapist been instructing mother in childrearing practices, the therapist would have taken credit for mother's effectiveness rather than assuming that mother was quite capable of dealing with her children well when she was free to do so.

It was decided to do something special in the fourth interview, involving a paradoxical ordeal. In all therapy the task is to have the person "spontaneously" behave differently, not behave differently because she is told to. One wishes the person to take the initiative for new behavior. In this case, the therapist's goal was to have the mother behave competently, not behave incompetently to make father feel needed. However, if mother were to behave competently because she was told to do so, she wouldn't be achieving the therapeutic end. One way to achieve that goal is to provide an ordeal of such a nature that the person "spontaneously" changes rather than continue the past behavior in the sequence. Then the new behavior does not occur because the therapist told the person how to act, but because the therapist inspired the person to take the initiative for new behavior.

The opportunity for a paradoxical ordeal occurred because the mother had been saying that father was better at dealing with the children than she was. Actually, she didn't seem to believe this was so and seemed to listen to the father's instructions to her as a way to help *him* rather than because *she* needed guidance. The therapist therefore set up a situation in which the father would be asked to instruct her in how to deal with the children, which was the arrangement they already had. However, to *require* that situation was an ordeal for the mother: It was necessary for her to sit with a professional woman she admired and agree to the idea that she could not deal with her children well and needed guidance from her husband. The more the ordeal went on, the more the mother was likely to demonstrate "spontaneously" that she could parent her children quite well without her husband's teaching and guidance. However, in this procedure there was no instruction from the therapist about *how* the parents ought to deal with their children.

The therapist set up the situation by saying, "Mr. Johnson, the next time your son acts up, could you supervise Mrs. Johnson to get him to sit down or do whatever he should do?"

"I could tell her, yes," the father said.

"Okay, when he does something wrong again, you help her step by step to get him to do what she wants him to do."

At that point the boy ran over and climbed on a chair, and mother said to father, "Make him sit down." This was the opposite of the therapist's request, since the mother was telling the father what to do rather than asking him what she should do. The therapist laughed, pointing out that instead of father supervising mother, she was instructing *him*. Father said, "Well, see, she does that."

The therapist once again asked father to supervise mother, and father chose to have mother tell the daughter to get down from a chair she was climbing on. Father said, "Tell her to get down off that chair." Mother said, "Come here, get down off the chair, get down."

"Tell her to get down," the father said.

"Get down out of the chair," said the mother.

"Call her to you. Tell her to come over to you."

"Come here, come here to me," said the mother. "Come on. Come to me. Come here. Get over here."

The daughter ignored the mother. Father set out to show mother how it should be done. After a few minutes of trying to persuade the daughter to do what he said, he gave up. The little girl managed to ignore both parents.

Finally the father said that he could teach someone, like his wife, how to parent, but "telling another person, they can't catch on that quick." The wife made her usual comment, "Like I say, there's some people can speak to a child once, mother or father, and the child obeys, where some kids don't. And mine don't. They don't pay me no mind. Now sometimes they do, not all the time. But most of the time they don't pay me any attention."

The therapist replied, "See, but now your husband's gonna help you."

"Oh," said the mother, appearing covertly angry, "he's gonna help me now?" The mother was being placed in a position where she had to be instructed in how to mother by her husband in front of a professional woman she admired. Such an ordeal forced her to rebel in the direction of more competence to demonstrate to the therapist that she was capable. As she showed that competence to the children, they responded by behaving better and even became willing to separate from her by staying in the waiting room with the toys while she was in the interview room.

Mother reported that a series of professionals had given her advice in the past. When she saw one of them again, "I'm gonna tell her that the method she told me is not working. And that we decided to listen to the people down at the clinic because they see the children every week." In the discussion it seemed that mother thought she was receiving advice about childrearing and parent effectiveness from the therapist even though she was not.

Besides helping the mother to be competent, the therapist helped her with her "nervous condition" by scheduling another paradoxical ordeal. Explaining to her that she was able to be only partially nervous and depressed because she was distracted by other things, the therapist said she needed a special time to be depressed. "You need to take at least ten to fifteen minutes a day," said the therapist, "and set it aside every day to be nervous and depressed. Get it all out of your way."

"Yeah," said the mother.

"At least ten to fifteen minutes a day. What time of day would you pick?"

The mother was helped to choose a time that seemed convenient—eight o'clock in the evening, just after the children were put to bed. That would be a nice time to relax and enjoy television, but now she must go through the ordeal of being depressed. However, on days when the children didn't misbehave and she enjoyed them, she didn't have to go through this depressed period. In this way the mother was encouraged toward more good cheer and competence with the children but without any instruction in how to do that.

Among the many paradoxical ways to offer a directive in therapy, one way is to simply ask the family to follow the sequence they came to therapy to recover from. In the seventh interview, the therapist framed such a directive as a way of helping the husband. She said that when the mother saw that the father was unhappy or depressed, she should get Arnold to misbehave and then be helpless to deal with him so that father would come out of his unhappiness and deal with the child.

"You understand what I mean?" asked the therapist.

"Yeah, I understand what you mean," said the mother.

"Repeat it back."

"You're saying to observe George," said the mother, "and when he is feeling depressed or down, to get Arnold to act up. Then for me to step out or go in the kitchen or something and let him try to quiet Arnold down. Is that what you mean?"

"Yes," the therapist said. "You act like you're not able to quiet him down."

By the next interview, the marriage was in trouble, as sometimes happens when a problem child is improving. It also sometimes happens as a response to a paradoxical directive. The mother arrived angry, and the children were screaming. Not only had father refused to come, but he had said his wife couldn't continue because they couldn't afford it. Discussing the argument just before she had come, the mother said, "He was so mad, I guess that's why he didn't come today. He went to work. He made me hot. He waited until I started ironing the baby's dress, and then he gonna tell me, 'Don't let him go no more, I don't have the money.' I told him, I said, 'He's gonna go if I got to scrub people's floors for him to go, he's going.' She began to cry and added that the clinic "has been doing wonders with this boy. But me, I'm the one that's neglected. I'm getting tired of it, I don't go anywhere. I'm in the house or sitting outside with the children. Not that my children is a burden to me, don't misunderstand me. I enjoy them too."

"I know what you mean," said the therapist.

"There's too much tension. I'm under too much tension, that's what it is."

"When you say that, you mean like how?"

"Like trying to do everything. And then he come in and just lay up on the sofa and don't do nothin'. And then he wants to know if his dinner is ready. 'Is my shirts clean?' "

Early in the therapy, the mother had said that she never went out anywhere, but she excused it by saying they had little money. Now she angrily expressed the idea that the issue was her husband's neglect of her. The problem for the therapist was that the couple's quarrel might escalate and they would separate, or they might withdraw from each other and again begin the sequence that would require the child's abnormal behavior. One step in changing the situation was to ask the mother to be nice to her husband when she returned home. Typically such a quarrel would continue, or the wife would withdraw angrily and become depressed. The husband could anticipate and adapt to her usual response. However, he could not respond in his usual way to a wife who was being unexpectedly nice after he had provoked her to be angry. He would have to change his response, and so the sequence would change. The therapist made the request quite directly. "I want you to be nice to him all this week," she said. "It's gonna be hard, with you being mad and everything, but I have a reason for you doing this. And we're gonna talk about that—how it went and why I want you to do it—next week when you come in. Be nice to him this week."

The mother agreed to be nice and apparently succeeded. The following week the husband came in with her, and the therapist spent some time alone with the husband.

"How do you think Mrs. Johnson is coming along now?" asked the therapist.

"She's doing fine with the kids now," said the father. "I do give her that much credit. They understand her. They don't holler when she tells them to shut up. They'll just look at her and pout."

The therapist asked whether it had helped to come to the clinic, and the father said "Oh, it helped a whole lot." When asked about improvement in the daughter, he said she too had improved. He never had to threaten to spank her. He added, "Being around all them kids in the waiting room has helped. I bring them down here, and both of them know right where them toys is."

By this tenth interview the presenting problem was essentially solved. The boy's yelling had stopped, the temper tantrums were over, and the children could be taken to public places without any misbehavior. The parents were negotiating for a nursery school for the boy, and intelligence testing was being done to determine whether he was limited. The therapy was not yet terminated, but it could be said that the experiment had been successful. Without any education of the parents in childrearing practices, they had become effective parents and the goals of the therapy had been achieved.

Although parent/child relations had improved, there was still a problem in the husband/wife relationship. The couple seemed to express little or no affection for each other. It was decided to take steps to improve the marriage even though they didn't wish to discuss their marital relationship. They were asked to change their behavior "for the sake of the children." This represented a deviation from the experimental plan, since a childrearing issue was discussed with them. The parents were asked to express affection for each other so the children would learn more about how to show affection (even though the children seemed to behave in normally affectionate ways with the parents).

This relatively mild suggestion, in preparation for giving a directive, aroused objections from the father. "That's for young people," he said. "I've been married for five years, and I'm used to my wife." He added that kissing was nasty because it spread germs (this statement surprised the therapist, who said that she'd heard of people who had that idea but she'd never before had the opportunity to meet one). The mother contributed an objection by saying that she was always embarrassed about showing affection.

After considerable persuasion by the therapist, the couple agreed to show affection for each other regularly each day. Every hour on the hour mother would kiss father on the cheek, and every hour on the half hour father would kiss mother on the cheek. They followed through with this plan, and it seemed to free them from the impasse between them. From that point on they became more affectionate with each other.

The parents remained together, and the mother went to work. The boy successfully attended a nursery school, and later the daughter also did. A follow-up after a year showed that the improvement was continuing. The therapy took twenty interviews, although the last several were for testing and check-ups rather than specifically for therapy.

In this experimental therapy the parents were not educated in any ideas about childrearing, did not receive insight into the ways they dealt with their children, and had no reinforcement schedule or education in parent/child relations. With simple encouragement and several ordeals two very difficult children changed their ways, and parents and children lived together more harmoniously after the experience. The children did what the parents asked without temper tantrums, and they were able to be apart from parents and accept other people. These results suggest that problem behavior in children is a product of an organization rather than the result of parents who are uneducated in childrearing practices. It does not follow that parenting skills are innate or instinctive, but rather that parents are exposed to the information over the years from sources outside therapy.

Since parents expect to be talked to about how to raise children, a therapist should be courteous and have such discussions. However, talking about how to raise children and changing the behavior of a problem child are quite separate endeavors. At least that seems to have been so in this case of the children who fell out when parents were exposed to a series of ordeals rather than education in childrearing.

5

❖━━❖━━❖━━❖━━❖━━❖━━❖━━❖━━❖━━❖

He Never Had
the Chance

A mother called and said she wanted therapy for her seventeen-year-old son in the hope that hypnosis could solve his special problem. Sandy, a nice-looking youth, slim and athletic, arrived for the first interview. His problem was that when he spoke, he blocked on certain words and could not say them. This was particularly so on the telephone. He would talk normally until he blocked and then would struggle with a word, his face contorted. The effort ended only if he stopped trying to say the word, perhaps substituting another. For example, when trying to say he had returned to his house, he'd say, "I went to the how—how—how—back home." His problem was not a stutter or a speech defect. It was a difficulty saying words, with the effort to say them magnifying the difficulty. Terribly embarrassed by the problem, Sandy avoided conversation with strangers, was shy with girls, and almost totally avoided talking on the telephone. He said the problem was so bad on the telephone that he sometimes simply could not even say "Hello," and the caller thought no one was answering.

Talking with Sandy in the first interview, I watched him struggle with words and become frustrated when he couldn't speak. The words on which he blocked showed no systematic pattern. It wasn't that he could not speak words with sexual connotations or words that referred to his home or parents. There also didn't seem to be any special speech configurations that gave him difficulty. At times he could say a word, like "house," quite easily, and at other times he struggled with the word and gave up in frustration.

Sandy had particular difficulty when he needed to read something aloud. That had caused a problem in school. When he blocked on a word, he could read no further because he could not substitute some other word from his extensive vocabulary. The fact that the words were fixed on the page and he couldn't change them gave him an impossible situation. I had him read a paragraph from a magazine. Sandy struggled with words again and again as if it were torture. He simply could not read a complete paragraph. However, when I asked him to read the paragraph backward, Sandy could do it quite easily. This is not uncommon with people who block on words when reading. When the anticipation of having to say a word makes a problem, reading backward is possible because words are not easily predicted when the content of the sentence is unknown.

After testing the young man with talking and reading, I concluded that the youth had the ability to make any sound or say any word. The problem was not physiological but largely one of expecting a difficulty with a word and having that prophecy fulfilled. I hypnotized the young man. Sandy was a good hypnotic subject. He could achieve various trance phenomena such as having a hand lift by itself or developing anesthesia in a skin area, and he could visualize well enough to hallucinate a picture on the wall. He could also develop amnesia for the trance experience. Practicing different trance phenomena, I had Sandy talk about his experiences while they were happening. In trance the youth had only occasional speech

blocks, but he did have them. When given posthypnotic suggestions in relation to the speech, he would continue to have the
speech problem in a more modified form. Clearly Sandy had
his difficulty with speech even when under hypnotic influence,
and I was puzzled that hypnosis did not have more effect. It appeared that the problem had some special function and was
necessary. The young man was not going to give it up easily.

In the preliminary conversation, the young man had said
that he had an identical twin brother, Randy. His twin did not
have the speech problem. As an experiment, I said to Sandy,
while he was in trance, "I want you to begin to imagine that
your name is not Sandy. As you imagine that, you will begin to
realize that you are not Sandy. You will be puzzled, but not
particularly worried, about who you might be." I asked the
young man to shake his head "no" when asked whether his
name was Sandy. He did so, and an expression of puzzlement
and disorientation appeared on the youth's face.

"Now you can begin to realize that you are Randy," I
said. I added that it would be with a feeling of relief that he
would realize he was Randy. When the youth nodded in response to the question whether he was Randy, his twin brother,
I began a conversation with him about sports. The young man
lost his speech block, since Randy did not have one, and
chatted easily. After a while I reoriented him back to his own
identity and had the same conversation with him, and the
speech block returned. In two interviews with the young man,
and with considerable hypnotic suggestion, I found that the
only time the young man did not have his speech block was
when he was identified as Randy. At that time he could speak
as normally as anyone and could even read easily and talk on
the telephone. When he became Sandy again, the problem returned.

I asked the boy's mother to come in for an interview. She
was a pleasant, rather vague woman who talked about the difficulty of raising twin boys. She had always dressed the boys
alike, since it was cute. The boys were always encouraged to do
everything together. The family could tell them apart, but other
people could not, and the boys had often exchanged places in

school and had done other mischief possible with two look-alikes. If one of them did something wrong, both were punished, since probably the other had also been at fault. The parents seemed to have treated the twins like an undivided cell. When Randy had broken his leg and had had to miss so much school that he was held back a grade, the parents had also held Sandy back a grade so the boys would not be separated into different classes. The mother said the boys still did everything together. They had built their own version of a motorcycle, which they shared. Laughing, the mother said that recently they had even been dating a pair of identical twin girls, so that all their dates were together too.

As the mother told this amazing story of two boys treated as one, I did not criticize the ways she had raised the boys but had her talk about her experiences with them. She had wanted therapy for Sandy because the boys were going to graduate from high school that June and go off to college. She didn't want to see him handicapped with this problem in his new life in college. Of course the brothers had signed up for the same college.

When I asked the mother whether there was any way the boys were different from each other, she was thoughtful. Finally she said, "Well, Sandy has this speech problem where he can't talk at times, and that's different, since Randy doesn't have any problem speaking at all. In fact, Randy does a lot of the talking for Sandy because he is embarrassed by his brother's problem."

That week I invited Sandy to be a demonstration subject at a class I was teaching on hypnosis. It was an evening seminar for psychologists and psychiatrists, and occasionally I brought a client to demonstrate hypnosis for the group. Since it was partly a social occasion, it was appropriate to invite Randy to the seminar as well. When the boys arrived, it was really quite impossible to tell them apart—except for the speech problem.

As I hypnotized Sandy before the group, I observed Randy's responses. Not only was Randy concentrating on the specific ways Sandy was responding to the suggestions, but Randy also began to respond to the suggestions himself. While talking with Sandy, I would occasionally direct my voice toward Randy, and he too would respond. When finished with Sandy, I asked Randy whether he'd like to be hypnotized, and he was eager to participate. He seemed to not wish Sandy to have an ability or experience that he himself did not have. Randy proved to be an eager hypnotic subject, clearly determined to do as well as Sandy. He produced all the trance phenomena that Sandy had been able to accomplish.

That evening I discovered that when Sandy exhibited his speech problem in a conversation, Randy would quickly fill in the word for him. Then Sandy could repeat it. For example, Sandy would say, "We both like pee—pee—pee—," and Randy would say "peanuts." Then Sandy could easily say "peanuts" and go on with his sentence. They worked as a team, and Sandy managed to talk without too much difficulty when Randy was there to quickly cue him with the proper word.

I invited both twins to the next therapy session, asking Randy to join us to help his brother with his speech problem. During the interview the boys talked about the experience of being twins. They did not object to having been treated so much alike over the years. They thought that was natural with twins, and it was reasonable, since in all ways they were alike. As they put it, there was no difference between them physically, mentally, or in any other way. They had the same likes and dislikes and the same talents. In their discussion I learned that the twins ran the 100-yard dash at exactly the same speed, to the second. They high-jumped exactly the same height. They pole-vaulted to the same height. In swimming, they swam at exactly the same speed in each of their different types of swimming, which they did equally well. When I expressed surprise at the exact sameness with which they did everything, Randy pointed out that they were physically the same, and so that was to be expected. When asked what happened if one was better than the other at something, they said that he immediately coached his twin in how to do it so they could do equally well.

What became evident in the conversation was not merely that they did everything alike but that they were so competitive that they carefully avoided any competition. The rule seemed to be that one must not do anything better than the other. At the suggestion that one who might have done better—who could have run the 100-yard dash faster, for example—might be holding back so the other one could be the same, they both denied it. They said it was simply a matter of learning how to do it the same way, and then they would achieve the same speed. They both claimed to function at their maximum capacity and said they didn't restrain themselves to help each other.

Not only was there no difference between them in athletic events, but they got the same grades in school and were good in the same subjects. They both liked mechanical work, and they had built a complex motorcycle, which belonged to both of them. They both said they weren't serious about the twin girls they were dating, but it was amusing to have pairs of twins out together. Neither boy had ever been involved with a girl more than the other boy.

Despite the pleasure they had in doing things alike, their discussion also had an underlying tension when the subject of competition was discussed. They protested too much that they achieved everything equally, as if it took an effort to maintain this idea. Clearly there was some feeling that one had to restrain himself to be equal to the other, just as the other had to stress himself to achieve the same level of performance. The strain was evident in their conversation, but it was covert. Any suggestion that there was tension between them or that their attempts to achieve equality showed a high degree of competitiveness would have been stoutly denied. I made no such suggestion but merely marveled with them at their remarkable equality. By the end of the interview, it had become evident that the only difference between the youths was Sandy's blocking problem. They even shared that insofar as Randy gave Sandy the word to say when he blocked.

Toward the end of the interview, I said I'd noticed how nicely Randy helped Sandy with his speech problem by saying the word Sandy was trying to say. I said to Sandy, "You must really appreciate that." Sandy hesitated and then quickly said he did. Evidently there was an underlying issue that Sandy did not appreciate that help from his brother or needing the help.

I asked Randy whether he'd be willing to continue to help his brother, but in a different way. Randy replied that he'd certainly be willing to do whatever he could. I said that it might be something difficult that would make them both a little uncomfortable. Randy said he would still be willing as long as it helped his brother.

"All right," I said, "here is what I would like you to do this week. When your brother has trouble saying a word, I want you to help him as you have been doing. But this time I want you to say the *wrong* word. If he is trying to say 'peanuts,' and you see he is trying to say that, I want you to say 'pumpernickel bread,' or something like that. Could you do that?"

"I think so," said Randy.

To Sandy I said, "Do you think your brother is quick enough to give you the wrong word?"

"Yes," said Sandy, clearly showing, but not saying, that he didn't like the idea.

"Let's try one now," I said. "Sandy, tell us about something that happened this week."

Sandy began to talk, and he said, "So we went to the st—st—st—," and quickly Randy said "home."

"No, 'store,' " said Sandy, with irritation.

"Is that what you want?" Randy asked.

"Excellent," I said. "Go on, Sandy, let's do some more."

Sandy talked. It was a minute or two before he blocked on a word, and again Randy quickly gave him the wrong word. Sandy then quickly gave the correct word, just as he had in the past. It had seemed that he could say the correct word only if Randy said it first. Now it was clear he could say the word no matter what other word Randy said.

Congratulating Randy on doing so well, and saying he should do this even if it made his brother uncomfortable, I sent the two of them on their way, with an appointment set for both of them the following week.

That week I received a telephone call from the mother of the twins. She congratulated me on doing so well with Sandy, saying he just hadn't been blocking that week. The hypnosis was really working. The mother was pleased, and so was I.

When the twins came in for the next interview, I asked Sandy, "Well, has your brother done his job and given you the wrong word all week?"

"He never had the chance!" said Sandy, with an edge of triumph in his voice.

"That's right," said Randy. "He just hasn't blocked all week. I guess that hypnosis has worked."

"Well, I'm surprised it was this quick," I said. "Let's talk awhile, and if Sandy blocks, I want you to do your job."

I had Sandy talk about incidents in his life, discuss his future and what he would like to be, and generally talk about issues important to him and to Randy. Sandy did not block. I had Sandy read a page from a magazine. He started reading it backward. Then, with a smile, he read it forward without difficulty. He telephoned his mother to say he would be late for dinner, and he had no problem on the telephone.

I asked Randy to leave so I could talk to Sandy alone, and Sandy continued to have no problem either talking or reading. I congratulated him and said the change was remarkable. Fortunately, if he ever relapsed, there was hypnosis and also his brother to help him again.

I saw the boys together and separately over several interviews. I took an interest in their differences, and they began to talk about diverging interests. They sold their common motorcycle to get some money to spend in college. They began to date different girls. They also decided to go to different colleges. The problem did not return.

6

One More Time

Jerome Ford arranged an interview with a couple and their two children expecting a routine problem. Mother had called and said the ten-year-old, Dexter, was having difficulties and she was worried about him. The family proved to be an average middle-class family. The father, Henry, was a nice-looking man, age thirty-one, in a business suit and glasses. The mother was pretty, slim, and dark. Dexter was a nice-looking boy, and the eight-year-old daughter was pretty and bright. The family was white and the therapist was black.

After shaking hands with the parents and Dexter, the therapist said to the little girl, "And this is?" She replied, "Annabelle," and he said, "Write your name on the blackboard so I won't ever forget it." The girl happily went to write her name, and Dexter hurried over to join her and write his name too.

---

*This is the only case in this book in which the therapist does not impose an ordeal or the threat of one. There are two reasons for including it here. One, it illustrates how at times of crisis the therapy itself can be an ordeal which leads to a change for everyone, including the therapist. Two, I like the case.

93

As he made the family comfortable, Mr. Ford noticed that the mother looked so much in distress, biting her lips as well as her fingernails, that some comment was needed. "Are you upset?" he asked.

"A little, not much," she replied.

The therapist turned to the husband. "Is your wife upset?"

"Yes," the man said. "She's upset about this, and other things."

"Excuse me," interrupted the wife. "You mean the whole situation, not just at this moment? I'm upset about the situation, yes."

Continuing to talk with the husband, the therapist asked, "And other things, Mr. Edwards?"

"I'm sure," the husband said. "We have family problems, financial problems. I've been in three different companies that went out of business in the last year. It's taking all our savings. And my nerves—we haven't been getting along. It's a difficult time for a lot of people in the financial world, and it's been hard on me. I think I may be the source of a lot of it. I'm very upset. I want to find something secure, and she's been nervous, and my son—it's been difficult. I wanted to get some professional advice, to see someone. When I want to relax, I have to drink, and that's terrible." While the wife sat with her head turned away from him, the husband continued, "But it's good to know yourself, and I want to spend some time with someone myself. Because our family relationship is—if you don't have a job and you don't have a family, you have nothing, you just don't."

This long speech of the husband gave some evidence that this was not to be a routine case. The man was clearly as upset as the wife, and his voice quavered as he talked.

The wife made it clear that she was there for the child's problem, saying, "Can we openly discuss Dexter's problem in front of him?"

"Sure," the therapist said.

"Well, Dexter has problems relating to children his own age or older. He's afraid of them. He doesn't defend himself in situations where they are going to hit him or call him names and things like that. He gets hurt, but he doesn't want to do anything about it. Now with young children, or smaller children, he acts like a bully. He bosses them around. It's known in the neighborhood that Dexter hits smaller children. There was an incident where there was a little girl five years old."

"She's six," said Dexter.

"She's six now, well, all right," said the mother. "I don't know how much teasing she actually did to Dexter. But anyway, he wrote her a letter that I knew nothing about and dropped it in their mailbox. And the mother was very upset. She came to my house with it, and it was a very nasty letter. Things like 'die, die' written in it. You know, really morbid things he wrote to this little girl. And I—you know, he's not supposed to hit girls, he knows that. But he has—he does."

The description of a child's problem in therapy can often be taken as a metaphor about the problems of mother and father. If a mother says the child is terribly stubborn, one can suspect that later she will say her husband is stubborn. If the husband says his child never does what he asks, one can suspect his wife doesn't do what he asks. The therapist who encourages metaphoric expression about the child, and doesn't point out to the couple what they're "really" saying, gains a great deal of information about problems in the family without having to make them an explicit issue. Listening to this mother's description, the therapist might consider the hypothesis that there is violence in the family and father has hit mother. Perhaps people even wish other people to die. Such statements about the child do not always apply to the adults, but it is a hypothesis to consider. (And if the mother described her child in this way in a social situation, it would not necessarily mean the same thing. She is telling a people changer about the problem, and she will describe it in different metaphors in different situations.)

"I didn't know about this letter," the father said. "You should have told me about it. When did this happen?"

"A few months ago," the mother said, her face expressing her impatience with the father for not being more involved with their child's problems.

"You should have told me," he said. "We should have been here long before this if—maybe one letter is not enough. But I do know that he won't defend himself. He has the body of an eleven-year-old because he's about four foot ten, and he's been oversheltered. He thinks like a seven-year-old. I'm trying to build his confidence."

The wife interrupted, perhaps responding to the statement that her son was oversheltered. She said, "There are things that have to be said, right?" She turned to the therapist. "I've seen an attorney for a divorce. My husband—we're talking about Dexter's insecurity, and all, like he feels inferior. Now Dexter hasn't had a father, literally, for nine years. And I attribute a lot of the way things are developing with Dexter to this. I mean, all the other boys in the neighborhood have had their fathers out with them playing ball, or going places. Dexter hasn't had any of these."

"Until recently," the father said.

"Yes, until recently," she agreed reluctantly.

The therapist has found himself in new and unexpected territory. It isn't that mother and father argue about whether father should do more for the child, which often happens with children's problems. What is unique and a serious difficulty for a therapist trying to resolve a child's problem is mother's passing statement that she has filed for a divorce. The therapist has to know what the situation between husband and wife is before he can help them deal with their problem child as mother and father.

"Job pressures," the husband said, excusing himself for not being a father to the boy. "Just phenomenal, the pressures, or whatever. But it's something I've recognized. Something that has to be done. I can see she's right, in a sense. I've been home at night, and whatever, but I've always been preoccupied with the job, to the point where I just wanted to become supersuccessful. Then I wind up with nothing after going after everything. So recently I've recognized Dexter's problems, and we have been spending time together."

The mother, impatient with the husband's comments, said to the therapist, "If his father calls in the daytime and says he wants to take him someplace, Dexter will say to me, 'Mom-

my, I don't want to go.' I'll say, 'Well, that's all you have to do
is tell daddy,' but he won't."

"Are you two separated right now?" asked the therapist.

"No," said the father quickly.

"We're living in the same home," said the wife, "but not
as man and wife."

"You're not sleeping in the same bed."

"Right," she said.

"That's it," said the father. "I'm working on it—but
whatever."

The father turned to the boy and asked him whether he
had had a good time the night before, when they went to visit
the grandfather. The son said not much. When the father asked
whether he didn't want to go "because you were tired or because you just didn't want to be with me," the boy said, "I just
didn't want to be with you."

"I thought you really liked me," said the father.

"I do, but I didn't want to go."

The therapist said to the father, "You're working very
hard at—I don't know, I'm not sure at what. Maybe you're
working *too* hard."

"Well, I could be overdoing it," said the father. "I'm
working at two things. The most important is to build up his
confidence, personally, in himself, and second is to build a relationship with me. I am overdoing it, because it just hit me all of
a sudden," he touched his palm to his forehead, "she says she's
going to an attorney, and I looked around and I said, well, all
these years I dealt—and one time I did have something, in terms
of success, a certain amount of stock, or whatever. But it all
went down the tube, with a lot of other things. I just lost sight
of her. I took her for granted, and then she says she's going to
an attorney. Oh my, but my son is what has to be done. If I put
the same resources to him that I put on the job, I feel it would
be worthwhile, but it's going to take some time."

"Mm-hm," the therapist said casually. He turned to the
little girl, who was behind him opening a pack of gum. "Are
you going to give me a piece, too?" She offered him one.
"Thank you."

The son went quickly to the mother to get some gum and

gave a piece to the therapist, who thanked him. "Can I have this? Thank you."

"He's overgenerous, he tries to buy his friends," said the father. "I've done that all my life too, because I came from a broken family."

The therapist turned back to the issue of doing something about the son when the father said, "We are going to do something about his problem." The therapist said, "Who is the 'we' that is going to do this?"

"Myself and Mabel," said the father.

"As mother and father," said the therapist. He turned to the wife. "Is that what you want? My question is, Mabel—you can call me Jerome or Jerry—my question is: He wants to be a father to his son, and that doesn't mean, you know, that he is going to be a husband to you."

"Right."

"That's different, he's just talking about that one thing. Do you agree to that?"

"That's what I've always wanted, him to be a father to his son, regardless of what *our* relationship is."

"Yeah, and that's kind of strained right now," the therapist said.

"Very strained," said the mother.

"It's going to be kind of difficult for you to separate one from the other."

"No, I've made up my mind what has to be done," the father said, his voice quavering with nervousness. "There's no other way, I've got to have her."

"You've got to have her to do what?" asked the therapist.

"I just got to have her. I'll work on my son, I'll use him as a vehicle to attract her closer to me. Then by sharing, she will have something with me, instead of me getting involved in some stupid something on a computer that soon becomes obsolete, or whatever."

With irritation in his voice, the therapist said, "So you're saying that you're going to use your son to get to your wife."

"Mm-hm," said the father.

"Why not use Annabelle?"

"Well, she's probably neglected too, to a certain extent, but he's the one I see the most immediate need, you know—maybe I'm just being monolithic in my thinking."

"No, you're not that. You're just getting ready to mess things up," said the therapist. "I'm not dumping on you, I'm just going to call the shots like I see them, all right? And I believe you when you say that you're going to use your son to get to your wife."

"No, I've been giving it to her straight, too," the husband said, reaching out and touching his wife's arm. "I've been doing everything, since I noted . . ."

"I don't think you have," said the therapist. "I really don't think you have. I don't think it's been working that way. I'm asking you now, both of you, to just try to have it happen beginning right now—that you're a father to your son, but that's not to use him to get into a husband-and-wife relationship."

"No, I didn't mean that," the husband said. "I think I misled you there. What I was saying is I see her as a distinct problem that has to be solved with another set of ground rules. With him, I made up my mind to be the dad, but it's a by-product. We can share something—her and I haven't shared a lot. They are separate problems that have to be solved separately. I know what they are, thank God. At least I've learned more over thirty than I ever knew under thirty. Fortunately."

The wife said, "But he's telling me there isn't any way—that he can't do anything. As a matter of fact, he's threatening suicide. This is a very serious problem. He doesn't care about anything—the children or his job or anything."

"And you're biting your nails," the therapist said.

"I always have since I was a kid," she laughed.

"One of the things I was going to ask you for today," said the father, "is some sort of referral to someone, because I'm very upset."

"Yes, I know you are," the therapist said.

What was presumed to be a routine child problem has become a complex situation for the therapist. The wife has filed for divorce, while continuing to live with her husband. He is drinking and threatening suicide, and both husband and wife are visibly nervous and upset. The boy's problem reflects this desperate circumstance, and it seems improbable that it can be solved until the issue with the husband and wife is resolved.

The therapist faces a problem that often occurs in therapy. When a married couple arrives with a threat of separation, the therapist can encourage the separation or try to hold them together. It is impossible to be neutral and not influence the couple in one direction or the other, because every statement of the therapist exerts an influence. The therapist needs to decide which way he should try to help them go—either apart or together. The conservative posture is first to try to bring a couple together. If that fails, they can still choose to separate. Although therapists like to have the freedom not to have to hold couples together when they're miserable with each other, still the most helpful posture is to maintain the integrity of the relationship existing when a couple come in still living together. If their relationship becomes too miserable, then of course separation is the option. At this point, the therapist is trying to make up his mind in which direction to guide the couple. He is being influenced by the state of the children's problems and by the husband's threat to attempt suicide if his wife leaves him.

The mother described her decision to divorce in more detail. "In making my decision, I was very upset for three months. Until I came to some decision. And I put my children before myself, and that's how I made my decision. Because it's a very difficult thing to do. I was the way my husband is now. In fact, I'm still pretty nervous about the whole thing. You know, you feel like crying, and things like that."

"Right," said the therapist.

"And I'm taking tranquilizers and depression pills from my doctor, and that is helping me."

Gesturing to her husband, the therapist said, "How is he?"

"I just said, he's telling me—I don't like to talk about this in front of the children."

"They know most of it," the therapist said, turning to the boy. "You know most of it, don't you?"

"You don't miss anything, do you?" said the father to Dexter.

The therapist offered the parents the option of sending the children to the waiting room, and they did so. Alone with the therapist, the wife continued to express her concern about the husband's suicide threats.

"I'm very concerned and worried about him. Because he talks about suicide and says he's going to kill himself. I had tranquilizers, and he took the bottle of tranquilizers. I didn't see him take the five he said he took, but he said he took them. He keeps talking about suicide. He wanted to talk to someone—a doctor, you know—and I really think he needs to. I don't know if it is all acting, you know, to try to keep us together. Or if he really would do something to harm himself—I don't know."

"Why don't you ask him?" the therapist said.

"Let me just explain the context of what happened," said the husband. "I'm not rationalizing or justifying anything . . ."

The therapist interrupted him: "Your wife is going to ask you something."

"Okay," said the husband.

The wife turned to him. "Would you really kill yourself if we divorce?"

"I would have no positive reason to—I would care less about living."

"Would you kill yourself?"

"I did take those tranquilizers hoping I would get rest right away. The by-product was that I slept a little longer. I think you'd have to be crazy to actually kill yourself . . ."

"Would you kill yourself? You don't have to be crazy."

"I wouldn't care enough to do anything. I wouldn't care enough to work. I would probably seek relief any way I can. Probably drink too much."

"You drink too much now. And that hasn't helped anything."

"Well," the husband said, his voice quavering, "when you're in terrible pain, sometimes very short relief is enough to keep you—even if the next day—you're getting away from it, you're escaping, you're a coward and all that . . ."

"I understand why you drink, you know, you still didn't answer my question, Henry."

"I think you'd have to be crazy to say definitely, 'I'm going to commit suicide,' but I've seen people take years . . ."

"Have you felt like committing suicide?"

"I felt like there's no—absolutely no reason to live." Turning to the therapist and referring to the episode with the tranquilizers, he said, "If I might just tell you the context of what happened."

"Not yet," the therapist said.

"Sure."

Once again the therapist has decisions to make. If the husband is suicidal, the therapist must take action and hospitalize him if necessary. Yet even that decision is not a simple one, because a therapist must think of the consequences of hospitalization. This husband is in danger of losing both wife and job, and hospitalizing him at this time could increase his chances of losing both and so increase his motivation to commit suicide. The therapist decided to emphasize the positive aspect of the situation. Turning to the husband, he said, "Now tell your wife that you're not going to kill yourself."

"Just deteriorate," said the husband.

"Yes, you're just going to kill yourself slowly. Day by day."

"Well, that's what he's been doing," said the wife.

"Until something happens, right?" the therapist said. "Something happening, or beginning to happen, means really doing something about how you feel, all right? And the situation you're in. This is why you're here."

"Okay."

"So that somebody can begin to work with both of you, so we can begin to put the skids on this and arrange it so that you feel better about some difficult times that both of you are going to go through. That's why you're here. That's why you're not going to kill yourself. We may slow it down. How old are you now?"

"Thirty-one."

"Well, you'll die when you're seventy-one, we'll slow it down. Okay?" The therapist turned to Mabel. "Your husband is saying to you he's not going to kill himself."

"I don't fully believe that," she said. "He's brainwashed me to think that way."

"This Saturday her sister came over to take them out," said the husband, "and it crushed me to see them go out and leave me alone."

"I'm filing for divorce. Things are different now, Henry. Now I don't want to go with you. Before I wanted it, I needed it. Right? And you were never there."

"You've convinced me, I don't know any better."

To the therapist, the wife said, "This has been a repetition of my life—our lives—ever since I've known him, about thirteen years."

"Thirteen years?" said the therapist.

"We've been married for ten years."

"Ten and a half," said the husband. "There's just one thing we can't bring up, or it will go on for a thousand years. It could never be solved. I am just reconciled to swallow it. Don't ever bring up her family."

The mother said loudly, in exasperation, "That has nothing to do with it, Henry!"

"That reaction was enough to indicate what I mean. I'm taking one hundred percent of the blame. I'll absorb that."

The mother turned to the therapist and said firmly, "I feel I do not want to discuss our marital problems, because I came here only to help Dexter. As far as I'm concerned, I've made a decision, and there isn't anything right now, you know, that would make me change my mind. He said he's willing to work at this and that—it's just promises, like I've had for ten years and even before we got married."

Searching for something positive in the situation for the couple, the therapist brought up their past, hoping to find a time when things were going well. "Tell me," he said, "ten years ago, when he was twenty-one—how was it then?"

"It wasn't good then either," the mother said angrily. "I broke it off. We weren't going to get married. I said, 'Well, this is it.' And then what he's doing to me now, he did to me then. The crying and, you know, making me feel so sorry for him. I have feelings for him, I always will. But I feel this is it, I don't want any more marriage, and he starts this crying and makes me feel very, very sorry for him. He gives me all sorts of promises that he probably believes he can keep, but he doesn't. It's just too many times. We were separated for a year and a half.''

"A year and a half?'' asked the therapist.

"Almost two years. I came back to him and things were worse than when I left. He made things so rotten for me, it was like he was paying me back for the year and a half I stayed away from him.''

"Unfortunately, there are two things that are important,'' said the husband. "One is the turmoil with jobs about the time she came back. The whole financial community started to deteriorate, and I suddenly had no job. Two, I've given so much to my business world, and I have so little to show for it now. I'm convinced that was a bit of a waste.''

The wife gestured in exasperation. "I said to myself before I came, 'Oh, we're not going to talk about this.' ''

"Well, we need to get things clear about where things are,'' the therapist said. "It needs to become crystallized for all of us.''

"I guess the biggest issue,'' the mother said, "is that I am afraid of him. If I speak in a certain tone of voice, I might get a punch in the arm. I can't—you know, he drinks a lot, and he's hit me for the last thirteen years, even before we got married. He was drinking one night and he came home and I was in bed sleeping. He got a strap and he started beating me with the strap.''

"How many times did he hit you?'' the therapist asked.

"With the strap? I couldn't tell you.''

"Four times,'' the husband said.

"Henry! *I* know, *you* don't know.''

"I've been ashamed of it ever since.''

"It was not four times,'' said the wife. "It was a lot of times. You kept saying, 'One more time, one more time.' Anyway, that scared the hell out of me.''

"And I'm terribly ashamed of it.''

"Let me finish. The next day when I tried to talk to him about why, he says it was a way of expressing passion. Now for me this is, you know, like sick. And then he tries this again. I was in bed sleeping and he came home one night, he goes into the closet and gets the strap, and he says to me, 'Are you ready?' I says, 'Ready for what?' Then I realized what he had in his mind, and I ran out. I don't know where I got the energy to run as fast as I did to get away from him. I had to run to one of my neighbors' homes. So between that, I—there have been months, at least four months, where I have been petrified in my own home, not knowing what time he's coming home and in what condition he's going to be. I used to take all his belts and hide them. I lay in bed, and as soon as I heard the front door and knew he was coming in, I'd get pains in my chest, pains in my stomach, and you just can't live like that. I'm really afraid of him. It's not just when he's drinking. He has a bad, bad temper."

Listening to this description, the therapist must add the information to what he has seen and heard and continue to make a decision whether to try to hold the couple together or to help them separate. For some therapists, the episodes of violence would be enough to cause a decision to help the couple separate. Other therapists would not find this sufficient and would think the violence might be eliminated and the marriage succeed. This particular therapist continued to think in terms of first trying to hold the couple together. He talked to them about the possibility of working on issues between them, and he suggested it might take some time. The husband would have to change and offer his wife what she wanted rather than what she didn't want. Being ashamed wouldn't help; what counted was doing something different.

"He completely dominates me," the wife said. "I'm even afraid to talk to him in a certain tone of voice."

"Well," said the husband, "she just put me in my place."

"By filing for the divorce," the wife said.

"She shocked the hell out of me, going to that attorney."

"We were separated a year and a half, Henry."

"I thought you were back for a thousand years, and . . ."

"I didn't say directly to him, 'Henry, I'm going today for a divorce,' but I told him, 'Henry, you don't give me any alternative, this is what I'm going to do.' Because I told him to stop the drinking, and scaring the hell out of me and the kids."

"How long have you two not slept together?" the therapist asked.

"Two weeks," said the husband.

"Two weeks," the wife agreed.

"That's not very long," the therapist commented.

"An important thing is I recognize Dexter's problem," said the husband, "and I'm working on it and she knows it."

The therapist interrupted, "Mr. Edwards, Dexter is not in here now, and I don't want you to bring him into this conversation. That's part of his problem."

"All right," the husband said.

The therapist, still believing he might reconcile them, asked for some time to work out the issues between them, without an agreement to set aside the divorce proceedings at this time. He hoped that in a week of daily sessions he might make a basic shift in their relationship. He told the wife she shouldn't stop doing whatever she was doing about the divorce. "That's for you to decide, I have nothing to do with the decision to divorce or not to divorce." He added, "But I would like the three of us to meet right here every day this week. For one hour right here. At the end of the week, we can decide what we will do."

The husband was pleased with this idea; the wife was not. "Mr. Ford," she said, "I don't want to give my husband false hope. I feel I've made up my mind."

"Well, just food for thought," said the husband. "How can you make up your mind to divorce me and still live with me?"

"What do you mean, still live with you? Where can I go until this thing is settled?"

The therapist intervened, saying, "That's one of the things we need to talk about. Just those kinds of things. You know, if you are going to separate or divorce, how are you going to do that? So it works for you and it works for the kids."

"Well," the wife said, "I want to do what will help my children."

"I want to help them, too," the therapist said. "And I see your son as being very caught up in all of this."

The therapist interviewed the couple twice over the next two days. He talked to them about their relationship, encouraged them to do some new things together to start a different kind of behavior between them, and tried to resolve the difficulties between them. After the third interview he felt he was not producing any change. The wife was adamant about continuing with the separation despite the improvement in mood between them.

Uncertain how to proceed, the therapist called in a wise consultant to observe the next interview through the one-way mirror and offer advice. The consultant observed and concluded that the wife wouldn't go back with her husband even if issues between them improved. She was determined to separate. The consultant advised the therapist to see the wife alone and ask whether she was still determined to separate. If she was, the therapist should shift and help the couple separate. The consultant and the therapist were worried about the husband's drinking, violence, and suicide threats. It was a provoking and dangerous situation for the wife to threaten a divorce while living in the same home with a man with a history of violence. If the therapist didn't take action to prevent the possible violence, he was contributing to it. The consultant suggested that if the wife was determined to leave, she should leave with her children that very day. She should not go back into the house with her husband after telling him she was finally leaving him.

The therapist interviewed the wife alone and said, "I've said that getting a divorce—separating or continuing with your husband—is really up to you. We've been at it for several days now. And I think it's time to ask you what you want to do."

"My plans are the same," said the wife. "I'm going to continue with the divorce."

"You will continue with the divorce."

"Yes."

"Okay."

"Now Henry has been promising all sorts of things and promising changes. I've told him I feel exactly the same. He says anything's possible, and he thinks I might change my mind if I see all his changes. But I really don't know that I would ever change my mind."

The task for the therapist at this point was to help the wife carry out her decision to separate in a way that was best for everyone. A couple who had separated before and gone back together could be expected to have difficulty going either way. One would expect that if the therapist changed his position and agreed with the wife that she should separate, she would begin to have doubts. For years she had been unable to leave her husband when she wished to, even when he hit her, and so it could be expected that the separation would not occur easily.

When the woman expressed her determination to divorce her husband, the therapist said, "Then you should go about the business of arranging the separation and divorce, and make plans for you and the kids, right?"

"Yes," said the wife, "but I'm very worried about my husband. He's thinking positively. He really feels we are going to be together."

"Well, you will be, on some things."

"No, I mean, you know, living as man and wife. I don't think he believes me yet, and I'm worried about it."

"How do you mean—worried?"

"I feel he's emotionally unstable, and that, you know, the threats of suicide and all, I'm really worried about that. I think he would be capable of hurting himself, because he is very upset."

"So what do you think you can do?"

"I really don't know what I can do. I don't know what to do."

"Well, you could stay with him."

"You mean as his wife?"

"Yes."

"I can't do that."

"Okay, so you're not going to do that."

By emphasizing how she could stay with her husband and having her decline that option, the therapist confirmed her more in her decision to separate. He also mentioned that this was the second major separation between them, and this time she seemed to really want to do it.

"Yes," she said, "although it's hard for me."

"I understand that. Well, if you stay with him because you don't wish to hurt him, and you feel sorry for him, then it's going to be rough for you. It's going to be almost impossible to stay with him that way."

"Yes."

"If you separate from him, you know, which you have done in a sense because you aren't giving as much as you were, you'll be withdrawing from the marriage. But to continue to live with him when you don't want to, that's a bad situation for you and for him. When you decided to file for divorce, what kind of separation was in your mind?"

"A divorce. Because I've tried just separating before."

"Okay."

By commenting that she had already begun to separate, and by emphasizing the finality of the separation, the therapist was encouraging her to move toward that goal. As she did so, she also had to bring up her doubts to be resolved.

"It's a funny thing," she said, "but when we're apart, like if I'm out with my sister and her husband, I think of Henry and I wish he could be with me. You know, I have so many mixed feelings. Then when I think about it really seriously, I know I have to do it."

"Because Henry won't really be with you the way you would like Henry, or some other man, to be."

"Right. I'd be very grateful if you would continue to talk to Henry and help him."

"I'm not going anywhere, you know," the therapist said. "I'm going to be right here with you and with the kids and with Henry."

"Okay."

"Now I'm going to ask you to do something that is drastic, but it's going to help. Okay?"

"Mm-hm."

"You're going to have to pack up your things and take yourself and your kids and go."

After a pause, the wife said, "The only place that I could go is to my mother and father."

"Right."

"I thought maybe we could stay in the same house until it was final. You know, sell the house, and then I would have the money to go and live where I wanted to live with the children."

"Well, I don't think it can be that way."

"Right. I think it's hurting me more than it's helping me, you know, watching him." After a pause, she added, "My son, Dexter, I don't know, in the last few months he seems to resent me a lot. He answers me back. It seems to me like he's blaming me for everything that's happening."

"Well," the therapist said, "it's going to be different for him, too. But let's take one thing at a time. You start talking about how bad it's going to be for the kids, and heap that on top of what you have to do, and you may find yourself paralyzed again—not able to move out of it. So I'm saying, you need to do one thing at a time. If things are going well with you, it's a good chance things will be okay with your kids, even though they're not living physically in the same place with their dad."

"Yeah."

"So if you were to pack your things and take your kids to stay with your mother and father, would they take you in?"

"Oh, yes."

"Okay. I need to bring Henry up here to talk with him. You want me to talk with him first?"

"All right."

"Why don't you wait in my office, I'll talk with him, and then I'll bring you back here."

A therapist who intervenes in people's lives should take responsibility for that intervention. After advising the wife to move out of the house if she was going to separate, the therapist had to be the one to tell the husband that that was going to happen. He should take the brunt of the husband's emotional upset, which was to be expected. After escorting the wife to wait in his office, the therapist brought the husband to the interview room for the difficult task of telling him that his wife not only had decided to leave him but was moving out that day.

To make the problem more difficult, the husband entered cheerfully, still believing things were going to work out. "I appreciate your staying after five o'clock today," he said to the therapist, smiling as he sat down.

"Okay, it's my job to do that," the therapist said. He paused and then spoke slowly and carefully. "I'm concerned about your wife and about you and about the kids. I'm more concerned about your wife and how she's feeling."

"Sure," said the husband.

"And about some very difficult decisions that she has to make. And you have to make some difficult decisions, today. We'll be together tomorrow to talk over some of these things." The therapist paused after indicating that the relationship would continue and he would see the man tomorrow. Finally he said, "Your wife has really made up her mind that she should leave."

"The house?" asked the husband.

"Yes," said the therapist.

Standing up, the man said, "Could I walk around a little bit? I'm just really upset. You mean leave the house?"

"Yes," the therapist said. He leaned back in his chair, becoming more casual in his movement as the husband became more agitated, pacing up and down.

"Before the divorce is over?" said the husband. "You mean leave the house? Maybe I'll just sit down." He sat down and passed his hand over his face, looking vague.

"She left the house before," the therapist said.

"Yes, but that's—I understood that—this time it would have been my fault. And it's the end. Did she tell you she was going to leave the house too?"

The therapist, who was ultimately obligated to tell the husband that he had advised the wife to leave the house that day, had the problem that if he told the man at that point, the man might become angry at the therapist or be hurt. It wasn't simply the anger that would be a problem; if the man left the office in anger, he'd have no one. The therapist would be lost to him as well as the wife. It was important that the therapist maintain a relationship with the husband while also being honest with him about the advice he had given the wife.

"Your wife has filed for divorce—," the therapist began.

"That I know, and that could be dropped within the next three months if I—if I tell her what I'm going to do. And I intend to do it. I've already made some decisions. Those decisions are made. If I have the right support—I know I'll do that. But did she say she's leaving the house before the divorce?"

"She said she would feel better."

"Oh, God, if she left the house, oh, God." He paced up and down more erratically.

"You have to let me finish."

"You have to say it fast."

"I can't say it fast. How can I say it fast?" the therapist said, his voice more firm as the man was more visibly shaken.

"I'm sorry, I'm just . . ." The man's voice trailed off.

"I need to say it to you, before you go off saying all kinds of things, and thinking all kinds of things."

"All right," said the man.

"You need to listen to it and take it on the chin, but not feel as though it's the end of the world. Because it's only, you know, today. All right? It's not tomorrow, or any other day."

"Can I stand?" the man asked, getting up.

"Stand, walk around."

"If she looks at things the way they are right now," said the husband, pacing the room, "they are bad."

"I'm glad you said that."

"The last two weeks have been better, but if she gives me time to prove to her . . ."

"That's good, you're sounding better."

"Prove the things to her, then she's got it made." The man spoke as he might at a board meeting, emphasizing the points.

"That's good."

"She's got it made."

"Right."

"But she's got to stay with me. I'll do it for her. I made up my mind to that."

"That's good. That's a good position that you're taking."

"Right. It's positive."

"It's a positive statement."

"But I need her to help me."

"But she needs to have some room between you."

"She wants to go to her mother's?"

"Well, she needs to tell you what the arrangement will be. You two can talk about how it's going to happen."

"Well, I don't have any money to go on my own," the husband sighed. "In fact, they cut off our electricity today. Then the job is—like, there's no money this week for salaries. I mean this—this is on top—like the worst thing that could happen to a guy. When she's not there, I'm in bad shape. I have to, you know, go out and drink, just be around people, or whatever." He paced up and down thoughtfully. "I think she's wrong there. We have to work it out together, solve the problem together."

"I agree that we have to solve the problem together." The therapist stood and began to walk up and down with the man.

"Right. I feel like I'm in an elevator and it's closed on me. I'm on the twenty-first floor and they're all gone. I'm actually, like, having a phobia, frightened to death."

Looking at him closely, the therapist said, "You know, you talk like I'm not here. I'm with you."

"Well, I appreciate what you're doing."

"But see, your wife has decided to do this because she's going to feel better."

"I'll give her as much room in the same house as she wants."

"But that's not how she wants it. If it does happen, it doesn't mean that she's going to be gone forever, at all. It just means she's doing this for the time being."

"I don't know how the hell I'm going to survive, but that's my problem."

"Well, we'll be here tomorrow morning, whatever happens."

"Did she already leave?"

"No, I'm going to go get her. And then we can sit down and talk about it."

"All right, it's the worst thing that can happen to me right now. I don't have any possible alternative."

"Oh, yes, we're going to be together tomorrow, and we can talk about the alternatives then."

"Did she say when she was going to do this?"

The therapist paused. "I suggested to her as soon as possible, since she feels that way."

"Okay, but I got to have some support."

"That's what we're going to be doing in here."

"What about the other twenty-four hours—twenty-three hours a day? When it's really, you know, the real world, the rest of it." Taking off his glasses, he began to weep, rubbing his eyes with his thumb and finger. "I'm being a crybaby, forgive me, will you?"

"This is not easy for anybody."

"I know. Other people work things out."

"I'm not talking about other people, I want to talk about you. This is a tough time for you."

The therapist began to trap the man physically in the corner of the room. As the man paced, the therapist casually blocked his movement so that, more and more, he was restricted physically to the corner. The man appeared to be quite out of his mind for a few minutes, and the physical cornering seemed to structure him so that he pulled himself together.

"I think that if she said she needs more room," the husband said, "I'll give it to her in the house. Just having her around—"

"That's the way *you* want it, Henry, and it may not go the way you want it right now. But like you said, you have a plan where you can do certain things."

"Yeah, but I have no alternatives, you see. I just don't have any alternatives right now. It's just disaster, in more ways than one. It's just total disaster. I haven't really faced it." As he said this, the man was essentially pinned physically in the corner. He changed his vague look and seemed human and thoughtful.

"What do you mean?"

"What it would be like without her, you know. If I have the loss of her and the loss of a job. I know that I'm not capable of thinking right to even get a job. Then I'm nothing."

"You got me, Henry," the therapist said, gesturing to a chair for the man to sit down. "I'm going to help you with this."

The man's attitude had changed and he seemed quite normal. "Well, I'm a twenty-four-hour-a-day guy," he said. "I appreciate what you—as a matter of fact, I like you as a person, my wife knows that. But as I said, at that point, if that happens, it's beyond what I'm capable of . . ."

"I'll go get your wife," the therapist said, and he left the room.

Returning in a few minutes, the therapist and the wife sat down. The therapist said to the wife, "I told Henry about how you were feeling and the decision that you made to get some room between you two for the time being. I don't know how long you want to do it or how it's going to be. That depends on a lot of things."

"I don't—I don't know how to—," the husband said, beginning to cry, sitting in a chair away from his wife and looking at her reproachfully. The wife began to cry, too. "Well, forgive me," went on the husband. "When that happens, you know, I don't have an answer to that."

After a pause, the therapist said, "You don't have any answer to what, Henry?"

"I can do without her sex. I can give you more room in the house. Just be there. Somebody to come home to." He continued weeping.

The therapist said to the wife, "Can you tell Henry where you will be?"

"Yes, at my father's."

"I don't want your pity, I want your love," said the husband. "My alternative—I don't have any."

"Okay," said the therapist. "You do have one, you know."

"What's that?" he asked.

"You can recognize that your wife has—that there is some distance between you and that she's living someplace else for a while. That you know where to reach her."

"That's running away from the problem, that's not giving me a chance. It's the end of it."

"Henry," the wife said, "I thought we could stay in the same house, you know, until the divorce was final, but it just won't work out that way."

"Why not?"

"Because it's like—when a mother has to let go of her children—me being with you all the time is getting harder and harder on me. Like this morning, that was a very weak time. You came over and were hugging me and I found myself hugging back. I have feelings. Then when you leave and I think about it, it's just not right. The whole situation isn't right. I need to be loved, and all those things you're doing now, kissing me and hugging me . . ." She sighed.

"I think what you're telling me," said the husband, "is that you've not only made up your mind to go through with the divorce, but you're going to see it all the way through at your parents' house. You're going to sell the house, give me my piece of it, or whatever, which I could care less about. Then your life will have started two seconds after you leave. And you're trying to leave me with false hope, just to keep myself alive."

"You know you're loading it on her, Henry," the therapist said.

"I don't feel that way," he replied.

"Well, that's what you did. Now, Henry, let's take what you said one thing at a time." He turned to the wife. "Now, is it your intention to go to your mother's and stay there until the divorce is final?" The wife nodded that she planned that. "Okay, do you intend to put a sale sign on the house and sell it, and give him his share, which he doesn't want? Is that your intention?" When she nodded, he went on, "Is it your intention to give him no hope at all? I don't know what he means by that."

"No hope for a reconciliation," said the husband. "Where the divorce could drop dead before it goes through."

"Is there a chance that you can reconcile along the way if he makes some changes?"

"I can't believe he would really change," she said.

"So you're saying he needs to find some way to demonstrate a change to you over a period of time."

"That's right," she said. "Over a long period of time."

"Well, what kind of demonstration?" said the husband. "In other words, you're saying that a long period of time will be after the divorce, after the house, after everything else."

"That's possible, yes," she said.

"Well, what will stop it before the divorce? If you stay at your mother's till the divorce, what do you expect me to do?"

"You have Dexter and Annabelle to think about."

"Forget that," said the husband. "I'm a failure, forget it, I can't see past this, that's how I feel."

"Okay, you can feel any way you want," the therapist said. "But you still have Dexter and Annabelle."

"That's not enough," the husband said.

"Well, wait a minute," said the therapist. "Two days ago you were ready to do things with the kids and demonstrate how you were going to be a father, which is part of what she wanted."

"That's a separate problem," the husband said. "I saw myself doing it, and I was doing it, but I can't even think of doing it now. With you not in the house and me coming around and picking them up, I just can't see past you leaving."

"What you're really saying," the wife said angrily, "is that once I leave, it's dead for you too. You don't care for them."

"I'm not playing on your sympathy," he said. "After you leave the house, I know you're going to get a divorce. The house is going to go, the children, and I don't care about anything after that. Anything. I can't see past you at all. That's it. That's the end of it." To the therapist, he said, "I was going to ask you for professional advice, or for tranquilizers, or whatever. I'd try that, but *with* her. I'll do it *with* her. I'd stop drinking tomorrow, right, but I've got to have a reason. I mean, I've got to have *something*, I need relief."

"Okay, now your wife said it's not just your problem. You have to make some adjustments, she has to make some adjustments. You've got a son, a fine-looking boy, and a daughter to take care of, a very active, sensitive girl. They're going to need you." As the husband started to interrupt, the therapist said, "Now let me finish. You were asking me for professional advice, and now you're going to tell *me*. Now your wife is feeling too that you're an important guy, and that your involvement with the kids is really necessary. I suggest that you don't do any drinking or taking any pills, and that your wife do what she is going to do, which is pack her bag and take the kids and stay at her mother's. And tomorrow night the two of you should have dinner together."

"Why?" asked the wife.

" 'Cause I think he needs it, and you might need it too."

"I think you're not being fair with me," said the husband angrily to his wife. "I say for two stinking months, even for one month. And you can knock out the sex. I'm asking for the children's sake and not for our sake. Just give me the chance starting right now, no drinking, no drugs, no nothing. Just knowing you're there, I've got it made. I would say this. You give me that two months, and I promise I won't touch a drop from this day on. I prefer to stay away from drugs too. You be my wife for two months and I think you've done right by everybody. Our marriage is destroyed, the kids are going, the house is gone, the career is gone, who knows. That's all gone, I guarantee that. All of it. For one month—I think that in a month you would see I'd be under enough strain that it would bring out the best and the worst. I think you owe it to yourself, to the children, and to me. And to your family. I think you owe it to God!"

After a pause the therapist said, "He's loading it on you."

"Only because I have no alternative."

"The alternative is that you take care of your kids as a father, and that you try to win your wife back by changing some of your behavior, and you continue to come here so I can help you with that. That's the alternative."

"No, I can't," the husband said.

"That's how I want it, Henry," said the wife.

"I'm not capable."

"Why not?" she asked. "Don't your kids mean anything to you?"

"Sure."

"Well, you can't stop feeling for them because I'm not in the picture."

"First of all," he said, "I won't be able to support them

after a period of time. I won't be able to effectively get a job. I know that I'm going to be drinking every single day for relief, or drugs, or whatever else I can get. I'm going to become a mess. Now I'm playing on you, I know, and that stinks, but you asked me, and that's where it is."

The interview continued and ended with the wife leaving to pack and go with her kids to her parents' home. The therapist talked alone with the man for a while.

The dilemma for the therapist was evident. What could he do with a man who was threatening suicide, who had been abandoned by his wife, who was losing his job, and who was going alone to an empty house with the electricity turned off? The man had no friends and no family in the area to turn to for support. The therapist could do the usual professional thing and say that he'd like the man to telephone him that evening, or he could say that he'd telephone to see how the man was doing. That seemed too little when the man was in such desperate straits. The other professional alternative would be to try to get him into the hospital as a suicidal risk, but that could make the man's problems worse.

The therapist did something unusual. He went out drinking with the man that night. The next morning at the interview with the wife and husband, the therapist said to her, "We went out last night."

"Yes, I heard," she said.

"We talked about a lot of things last night," the therapist said. "Right?"

"Right," said the man. "There was almost no continuity, but we talked a lot."

The therapist laughed and said, "Henry is a very interesting person. We talked about a lot of things. And I felt very comfortable with him," he said, partly referring to the situation of a black man and a white man going out to drink together.

"Yes, we had a good time," the husband said, appearing surprisingly calm in contrast to the upset of the previous day.

The couple negotiated the issues of the separation. The stress of the therapeutic encounter, which was the ordeal in this therapy, was essentially over. The therapist continued to see the family intermittently over a period of months. The boy improved, the daughter remained fine, and the husband and wife survived the separation and the divorce. A year after the divorce, the husband had married again. The wife had not.*

*There is a special poignancy in this case for those of us who were friends of Jerome Ford. He was involved in a personal ordeal at the time of this therapy. When he talked to the husband about prolonging his life to the age of seventy-one, he knew that he himself had cancer and so had little time to live. He died a year later.

7

Using the Great
Outdoors

Haley: The first evening we were here, you touched on getting two persons involved in an ordeal. Can you give any other examples of that?

Erickson: Yes. A woman came to me who was an alcoholic, a pretty bad alcoholic. She hid all her drinks. Her husband came home from the office every day, and they had a nightly battle, because she was drunk and he was infuriated. So I told the two of them here in the office that he could continue to come home every evening and laboriously try to figure out where she had hidden the bottle of whisky. She could take a gleeful delight in

This chapter is a conversation among Milton H. Erickson, M.D., Jay Haley, and John Weakland in 1961. It is presented verbatim except for minor editing. A summary of this ordeal was presented in Jay Haley, *Uncommon Therapy: The Psychiatric Techniques of Milton H. Erickson* (New York: Norton, 1973).

121

hiding it. My statement was, if he could not find it, she was entitled to empty it the next day. I let them play that game for a little while. It isn't a good game. But he didn't like that hunting, and she got too much joy out of it, penalizing him. But you know, my arrangement robbed her of the privilege of hiding it secretly. This was the purpose of the hiding. Not that guilty, shameful, sneaky hiding. So it took some of the joy out of her hiding her liquor.

Haley: He was hunting for the bottle before you asked him to do that?

Erickson: Oh, he used to rage around the house trying to figure out where she put it, and he was always so angry that he never did find it. And she always raged because he hunted for it. So it became this game of skill. I haven't seen her for a couple of months now. I got a letter last week from her detailing her joy in life, her husband's joy in life.

Haley: You brought them together in the interview when you gave the instructions?

Erickson: Yes. And her facial expression when I suggested a careful hiding of the whisky bottle and the reward. It was his if he found it, it was hers if he did not. But you see, they'd been doing that for quite a number of years anyway—twelve years.

Haley: Something seems to happen when it is done at the suggestion of someone else. It's a very different situation then.

Erickson: Yes. Her idea of weekend enjoyment was to go out in the yard, work with the flowers, and when nobody was looking, slip that bottle of whisky hidden in the ground up to her mouth. She really enjoyed gardening. She also enjoyed the whisky. The husband's idea of a good weekend was leaning back in an easy chair and reading *Business Week* or the *Wall Street Journal* or the Sunday *New York Times* from cover to cover. I had him buy a trailer and go up to Canyon Lake with her and go fishing—without whisky. He hates fishing, and she hates fishing. I stated that being out in the water there alone, in a small boat, no whisky, keeping her sober, would be good for her health. It would be good for her husband to be out in the open and getting some fresh air instead of stifling his nose in the newspaper in sluggishness and inertia. They are now using their trailer, *not* to go fishing in a boat; they go camping on a weekend, and they both enjoy it. She has been sober, and she is going to keep right on being sober.

Weakland: How did you pick the boating idea? Because generally we've had questions in mind about what sort of ordeal to pick.

Erickson: You see, they originally lived in the Middle West. I always ask a lot of random questions, and I found out that there was a lake region where she lived, and she hated lakes. I asked her about fishing; she hated it. I asked her husband; he hated it. Well, then that is all that was necessary.

Haley: You assumed that if they had to go through an ordeal, they would pull a switch and make it a pleasant trip instead?

Erickson: I justified it; it was out in the open. A little exercise, freedom from musty old books and musty old newspapers, and freedom from whisky. Open air, sunshine, exercise. So now it's camping. They've got that trailer fixed up to camp in all the available areas in Arizona.

Haley: Well, do you have any other examples where you involve two persons in an ordeal?

Erickson: A seventy-year-old mother came to me with her schizophrenic son. He was fifty years old. He irritated the life out of her by sitting and moaning and groaning. She would much rather go to the library to read and spend the day, but he bothered her so she couldn't. So I had her get a library book, drive her son out on the desert, dump him out, and drive three miles down the highway. She was to sit there and read until he ragingly had completed his walk. The mother objected to it the first day I suggested it to her. I told her, "Now, listen, your son is going to fall down, he's going to crawl on his hands and knees, he's going to wait out there to stir your sympathy. Take a deserted desert road where there will be no passers-by. He'll try to punish you by making you sit there and wait for five hours, but remember he's out there on the ground for that length of time. He'll get hungry." So the son tried everything, but his mother obeyed my instructions. He walked, sometimes three miles in one trip. His mother said, "You know, I'm getting to like this reading out in the open." He walked more and more briskly. He sometimes volunteered to walk. That way he was allowed to cut it down to a mile. [Laughter] But he's volunteering, you see. And his mother is astonished at his improvement. She had been advised by his brother, a psychiatrist, "Put him in a hospital, there's no hope for him." Mother didn't want to.

Weakland: Did you give that instruction to the mother alone, or was the son there?

Erickson: In the son's presence. Because I wanted him to know that I knew exactly how he could stumble and fall, and faint, and anything else he wanted to do.

Haley: How did she get him out of the car?

Erickson: She once picked him up by the nape of the neck and brought him in here. She's a very forceful woman.

Haley: Apparently. What you're doing is encouraging her to help her son just as she always has.

Erickson: Yes, but *this* way, not in that old, soft, maternal way. To help him in a way that someone else says is good for her son. I saw her recently, and she wanted to know when she could start him bowling. He would rather exercise by bowling while she reads than walk in the desert. So, you see, he is improving.

8

Only on Sunday

The therapist who took on the problem was John Lester, a tall, handsome young man. He approached the case with enthusiasm but also with trepidation because of the unusual nature of the problem and the many past attempts that had failed to solve it. When he talked with the mother, he found her to be a small, helpless-looking woman in her fifties who had four children and trouble with two of them. Her husband had been dead for a number of years. She acknowledged a drinking problem, and at times she was difficult to understand because her speech was slurred. She wasn't embarrassed about talking about her son's problem; she'd talked about it with a number of doctors in the five years that she'd taken him from place to place trying to solve it. The boy, a slim, nice-looking ten-year-old, seemed less concerned about getting over the problem than his mother. He passively went with her wherever she took him, but he expressed no special concern. For the previous year and a half he had been in therapy with a competent child psychiatrist who had finally said he could not solve the problem and had given up. The psychiatrist had tried a wide range of ways to help the boy. He had talked with him about sex at length, and he had used play therapy and interpretations to bring out the sexual dynamics behind the problem. He had also spent time with the mother and advised her about what to do and about what might be the cause of the embarrassing difficulty. He had told her not to nag the boy, to ignore the problem, and to have the boy's sisters also cooperate in not nagging him. He had set up a behavior modification program in which the boy was rewarded when he did not do it; like all the other interventions, that one fizzled too. Medication had been tried, as had tutoring to help the boy in school in the hope that doing better in school would cause the problem to stop. Instead, the boy also had the problem at school, embarrassing everyone.

Mr. Lester asked the whole family to come to the first interview, but only the mother and the problem boy, George, came, as well as a four-year-old grandchild. The grandchild's mother, Barbara, was supposed to have come, but, according to the mother, "She got a little piece of a job. She only worked one day, and they want her to work this evening." (Actually Barbara proved to be a more difficult problem than George. She was twenty years old and was obese because of compulsive eating. She would rush out and gorge herself on giant sandwiches whenever she was upset, which was often. On the street she was in trouble fighting in gangs, and her boyfriend was occasionally in jail. She had two small children whom the mother was actually raising because Barbara was irresponsible about taking care of them.)

After making the mother and George comfortable, the therapist asked, "Is this problem a thing you discuss freely in the house? I mean, is everyone in your house aware of it, or is it something that is hush-hush?"

"Oh, no," said the mother, "it's been something that— Barbara used to try to get after him, and his other sister, before she went away to school, used to try to get after him and tell him to stop, you know. Then we started to try not to nag him about it, you know, but just to remind him."

"I know it's kind of difficult for you to explain this over

again," the therapist said, "but it's very necessary. Take your time in doing it. I'd like to ask you what are some of the things you've tried to help George?"

"Well, really," said the mother vaguely, "the only things —the only thing we tried is the tutoring, and the medicine. He's been taking Dexedrine, I think it's Dexedrine."

"Anything else?" the therapist asked.

"Well, we tried giving him a dollar a week if he wouldn't do it, but soon I was borrowing money from *him*. Really, it seems there was nothing concrete. The medicine seems to help him relax a little, the medicine seems to help. But trying to find the answer, why he does it, you know?" She scratched her head and looked away vaguely.

The therapist said to the mother, "We won't discuss this problem here together. It will be a private thing between George and myself. Because he is a boy, you know. He needs—it needs to be private. I would appreciate it if you would not discuss it anymore. Okay?"

"All right," said the mother.

"Okay, George?" the therapist asked the boy.

"Yeah," said George, not showing much interest as he looked away.

"I might be able to help George," the therapist said. "But you're used to having this problem with him, and if it does cease, he will be more difficult to live with. What if it just stops?"

Thinking of what she learned in previous therapy, the mother said, "He's going to have to have an outlet."

"I'm wondering if *you* could stand it," the therapist said. "I mean you are going to be left there by yourself without doing the things you're doing now to prevent him. It won't happen anymore, you won't be able to do those things anymore, what will you do with yourself?"

"What will I do with myself?" asked the mother, getting irritated at the implication that all she had to do in life was try to stop the boy's problem. "Well, I can find plenty of things to do with myself."

Her irritation was a necessary part of the therapeutic procedure for this particular therapy technique. It was difficult for the therapist to confront the mother in this way, because he was being taught a nonconfrontive style of therapy. However, he had been asked to tell the mother she was going to become upset if the son improved, and so he was doing that. She didn't like that idea, since she had devoted herself for years to helping her son improve. But if the therapist takes that position firmly, the mother will set out to prove the therapist wrong by helping her son improve and then showing she did not get upset. In that way mother and therapist are working together to change the boy.

The therapist said, "George will just become a normal boy; he'll be harder to live with."

"I could put up with that," said the mother. "He has got to grow up someday."

Mother and therapist looked at each other thoughtfully, and the therapist eased the tension between them by saying, "Still and all, you have your grandson to take his place," pointing to the four-year-old on her lap.

"Yeah, I still have him," the mother said, looking fondly down at the boy.

The therapist said he would like to talk to George alone, and the mother left the interview room. The therapist sat down with the youth and said he wanted to talk to him man to man. "Tell me," said the therapist, "do you know of anyplace in your house where you can go and masturbate all by yourself?"

"Yeah," said the boy, with some interest.

"You know someplace? Where nobody will see you? Do you ever go there now and masturbate when you don't want to be bothered?"

"Sometimes," said George.

The therapist was asking the boy about private masturbation as a first step in the therapy. George's presenting problem was public masturbation. He did it in front of his mother and sisters, and he had done it at school. Although the masturbation was extreme—his mother said he had worn holes in the crotch of his pants and had been hospitalized once for blood in his urine—still the primary problem was the masturbation in public and without pleasure. If done with pleasure and in private, it would no longer be a problem; trying to arrange that was the first stage of the therapeutic plan.

While chatting with the boy, the therapist stood up and went to a desk. "Tell me, how good can you write? Can you count?"

"Yeah," said the surprised boy.

"Can you count real good?"

"Yeah, I can count," George said defensively.

"All right, I'm going to see," the therapist said, bringing over a pencil and paper and sitting beside the boy. "I want you to do something for me. Okay? Now, first of all, let me make something known to you. Now, this is strictly between me and you. Right?"

"Uh-huh," said George.

"Now you have to promise me. Can I trust you?"

"Yeah."

"Okay. Don't let me down. All right?"

"All right."

"I believe in you, you got an honest face. Let me see, how many days in a week?"

"Seven," said George.

The therapist made out a chart of the days of the week with the boy and marked the dates until the next interview. "Next Friday will be the seventeenth, right?" said the therapist. "It will be the last day that you have to mark down each day, right? Now you know what you have to do?"

"Yeah," said George.

"Now you explain to me what I want you to do."

"Every time I masturbate," said the boy, showing enthusiasm for the writing task, "I put a mark in this block."

"For each day, right? Every time you masturbate on . . ." He stopped, letting the boy continue.

"Friday, Saturday, Sunday, Monday, Tuesday, Wednesday, Thursday, and Friday."

"And what else. You remember to do what?"

"Don't let anybody know."

"Right," said the therapist. "Don't let nobody see you, hear? Don't tell nobody about our agreement, right?"

"Right."

"I'll give you this," the therapist said, giving him the list. "You keep this in your pocket, okay?"

"Uh-huh," said George.

"Here," said the therapist, "I'll give you a pencil."

At the second interview, the therapist talked to the mother and son together, and then he saw the boy by himself. When alone with the boy, the therapist said, "Hey, remember what we talked about? Did you do it?"

"I brought the paper."

"You did? Let me see it. I knew I could count on you, I really did." They looked at the weekly chart together, the boy quite evidently proud of his work.

"Here, hold that for me," the therapist said, offering the boy his pen. "Do you have an ink pen?"

"No."

"You can have that one."

"Thank you."

"You're welcome."

"This is how many times I masturbated," said George, pointing to the chart.

"Let's see, on Friday you didn't do it at all."

"Right."

"On Saturday you did it one time."

"Uh-huh."

"On Sunday you did it four times."

"Right."

"And then you hadn't done it Monday, you didn't do it Wednesday, you didn't do it Thursday or Friday. Right?"

"Right."

"Tell me, you did it more Sunday than you did Saturday. Why was that? Kind of bored in the house on Sunday?"

"Uh-huh. Nothing to do."

"Do you think you can remember, out of these five times, which time it felt best? On Sunday or Saturday?"

After a thoughtful pause, the boy said, "On Sunday."

"Felt better on Sunday, huh? The reason why I'm asking, George—you know I always like to explain things, right? I want you to know the reason for everything—you know, the reason

I'm asking is that it is important that you do enjoy it *all* the time, you know."

"Uh-huh."

Pointing to the chart, the therapist said, "See this one time right here that you did it on Saturday, and you didn't enjoy it, you know, you're just wasting your time. You could have been doing something else, you know. I don't think it's fair to you. Do you understand?"

"Yes."

"If I see you do this on Saturday and you don't enjoy it, I'm going to tell you, right? I'm gonna say, 'Look, George, you're wasting your time doing it on Saturday. Do it on Sunday.' " He held up the sheet and pointed with the pencil. "I'll tell you what, now that we decided, you know, the both of us, that Sunday is the best day, right?"

"Uh-huh."

"Okay. I think that would be better, don't you?"

"Yeah."

"Because it felt better on Sunday, right?"

"Uh-huh."

"Yeah, I think that would be the best time."

"Yeah."

"But I'll tell you something else, too, now that you're gonna enjoy it more, right?"

"Uh-huh."

"You should do it a little more. Okay? You should do it a little more 'cause you're gonna enjoy it. It wouldn't make sense to do it the rest of the days and you ain't enjoying it at all, right?"

"Uh-huh."

"You enjoy it more, so you do it more. Sitting around and you ain't got anything to do, shoot, you might as well go on and enjoy it more on Sunday, right?"

"Uh-huh."

"Okay, let me see, I'll give you a couple more lines here," said the therapist, marking the chart. "I don't even have to put any more down here because you're just gonna do it on Sunday, right?"

"Right."

"So, here. I'll tell you what to do now. Draw a line through Monday, Tuesday, Wednesday, Thursday, and Friday. Draw a line right through them because we don't need them no more. I want you to tell me, what day are you supposed to do it?"

"Sunday," said George.

"Now what about the rest of the days?"

"Leave it alone."

"All of them, right?"

"Uh-huh."

"Got your word on that?"

"Yes."

Shaking hands, the therapist said, "My man. Now, here is what you do. Now, you did it four times last Sunday, right?"

"Right."

"Now that you're gonna enjoy it, you know, you might as well go ahead and do it more. Right?"

"Uh-huh."

"Now for me, this Sunday, here's what I want you to do. I want you to do it eight times. *Eight* times, now." The therapist leaned back and looked at the youth thoughtfully. "So you might have to get up a little early to start, you know?"

"Uh-huh."

"What time do you get up, anyway?"

"About eight—nine—thirty," said the boy casually.

"You get up at nine-thirty?"

"Ten—eleven," said George.

"Boy, you have to get up early!"

"Twelve," said George.

"Anytime you get ready, huh?" laughed the therapist.

It was important that the boy had said he enjoyed masturbating on Sunday. This made it possible to focus the masturbation onto that day and encourage it within a framework of helping him enjoy it. By scheduling the masturbation, it would be possible to increase it so that it became an ordeal, but within a benevolent framework of encouraging the young man to enjoy it. When a day has been set, it becomes possible to punish the youth for masturbating on some other day by having him do it more on Sunday.

Although the problem was the focus of the therapy, it was important that the therapist and the young man talk about other matters so their relationship would include more than that one issue. The therapist asked the boy, "What kind of games do you play after school?"

"Well, let's see, I play tag," said George.

"Do you run fast?" the therapist asked.

"Yeah," said George.

"Who is the fastest runner in your neighborhood?"

"Me."

"Yeah?" the therapist said, admiringly. "I'll bet you can beat them all running. You got long legs, like I got. I got long legs, too. I move around pretty fast. Do you play football?"

"Uh-huh."

"You do? Do you play baseball?"

"Uh-huh."

"What sport do you like best?"

"Basketball."

"Basketball. You got a girlfriend?"

"Yeah."

"What's her name?"

The boy slid down in his seat shyly. "Sally."

"Sally. Is she pretty?"

"Uh-huh."

"Do you ever play Catch-a-girl-kiss-a-girl?"

"No."

"You don't play that? We used to play that."

The following week, at the third interview, the therapist talked with the mother alone to get a report on the boy's behavior. After chatting with the mother about her various ailments, the therapist asked, "Has George been masturbating in your presence or in the living room?"

"Yes."

"He has? Often?"

"About the same. But I didn't say anything to him about it. I didn't mention it."

The therapist sat back in his chair in disappointment. He'd thought the problem would be solved more easily, as he had a good relationship with the boy and they'd worked out their arrangement together. "Can you give me an idea when and where?" he asked. "Any particular time?"

"Since he's been home this week [there was no school], I noticed it during the day. When he was looking at television, or—he hasn't been out of the house too much. Yesterday was the first time he's really been out of the house. His sister took him out. I think all weekend he stayed in."

After getting this information from the mother, the therapist talked with the boy alone. Looking over the chart, he said, "Now explain to me, you know, exactly what you have here."

"That's how many times I did it."

"Eight."

"You did it eight times?"

"Uh-huh," the boy said, holding his hand over his mouth shyly.

"I can't hear you with your hand up to your mouth."

"Eight."

"Eight times. What time did you get up Sunday?"

"Nine o'clock. My sister got me up."

"She woke you up at nine o'clock? Why did you get up so early?"

"I don't know."

"Did you tell her to wake you?"

"Uh-huh."

"You told her to wake you up early?"

"Yeah."

"So you could get it all in? Very good." He shook hands with him. "Good man."

Later the therapist asked about what had happened on the other days. "Did you do it?" he said.

"Uh-huh."

"When was that?"

"On Monday."

"And any other times?"

"No."

"And why did you do it Monday?"

"I don't know," said George, whining in the usual way he

did when anyone tried to get him to stop masturbating, "I couldn't help it."

"I understand. Okay," the therapist said.

It was fortunate that the boy had not followed the instructions, since that was necessary if the masturbation was to be made more of an ordeal. He had masturbated on a day of the week when he had agreed not to, so he could punish himself by masturbating more on Sunday. As the number of masturbations necessary on Sunday increased, the boy would begin to rebel against doing the masturbating—instead of rebelling *by* masturbating.

"You said you did it on Monday, right?" said the therapist.

"Uh-huh," the boy said sullenly.

"And we had an agreement that you were just supposed to do it—" the therapist hesitated, and the boy said, "On Sunday."

"Well, because you did it on Monday," the therapist said, "I want you to do it next Sunday four more times than you did it this Sunday past. Understand?"

"Uh-huh."

Taking the chart, the therapist said, "Then after I fill this out, I want to explain to you exactly how—because I don't think you're doing it right. I want you to try—try my way, you know. It's just about like yours, but it's a little better, okay?"

"Okay," said the boy.

Reforming the way the boy goes about the masturbation is a way to make it more difficult and so more of an ordeal to be rebelled against.

Writing on the chart with the boy, the therapist said, "Now, how many times did you have to do it last Sunday?"

"Eight."

"Okay. Now, how many times do you have to do it this Sunday?"

"Twelve."

"Now, why do you have to do it twelve times this Sunday?" When the boy sat up, looking puzzled, the therapist said, "You forgot. So you won't forget—because you did it on Monday. Okay?"

"All right."

"Now, if you forget, I'll write it down here so you can see. Now why do you have to do it twelve times on Sunday?"

"Because I did it on Monday."

"Right. Okay, now, how many times do you have to do it Sunday?"

"Twelve."

"Where at?"

"In my room."

"Okay," the therapist said, putting down the chart and leaning back in the chair. "Now, let's get away from that for a minute and let me explain to you—tell you what I was talking about. Now, you said when you masturbate, you know, you take your zipper down and you put your hand in your zipper."

"Uh-huh."

"Or sometimes if you don't do that, you just do it without taking your zipper down," said the therapist, indicating just putting his hand inside his pants. "Right?"

"Right."

"Okay. Now, this Sunday when you do it, I want you to do it differently, okay?"

"Okay."

"Now here's how I want you to do it. I want you to unbuckle your pants and take your pants all the way off. Right?"

"Yeah."

"But you must fold them up neatly. You know how to fold your pants up neat? You know, put the creases together?"

"Yeah."

"And lay them on your bed. Okay? Then take off your underwear. Right?"

"Yeah."

"Fold them up neatly and lay them right on top of your pants. Right?"

"Yeah."

"Now, you gotta do all that, now, you just can't take them and throw them in the corner. You understand?"

"Uh-huh."

"Now go ahead, tell me what I told you."

The therapist had the boy review what he was to do and

to pretend to do it without actually taking his clothes off. Then he had him do it again, saying, "Now go through it again, from the beginning."

Giving a large sigh at the tedium of this procedure, the boy repeated, "Take off my pants, fold them up, put them on the side of the bed . . ." and so on.

Although the therapy focused on the boy and his problem, to deal with only one person when there is a symptom is like assuming a stick has one end. Obviously, if the boy was attached to his mother, the mother was attached to him. In the interviews, the therapist spent time with the mother orienting her toward a life of her own more independent of her children. By doing so, the therapist attached the mother more intensely to himself, thereby helping her to disengage from her son. The mother reported that as her children were becoming grown, she wanted to go back to school but was not able to because of trouble with Barbara, her difficult daughter. She had to come home from work and take care of Barbara's children. The therapist encouraged her to get into the school or job she wanted to get into and said he'd try to help her get Barbara to become more responsible.

At the fourth interview, the boy appeared more mature. He was on a hockey team and talked more animatedly. He also was beginning to show some rebellion. He did not bring in the chart. During the time alone with the boy, the therapist began to tie the second symptom that the mother had complained about, occasional thumbsucking, in with the masturbation. He arranged that the boy masturbate eight times on Sunday, and then he said, "Now, because you don't suck your thumb when you're playing hockey, right? And when you're reading comic books, you don't suck your thumb. I don't think it's necessary, do you? Not for a big guy like you, you know."

"Uh-huh," said George.

"Imagine, you get a girlfriend and you'd be sitting there and she may try to kiss you, and you got your thumb in your mouth. That would blow it, wouldn't it? Sure would. Look, when you suck your thumb during the week, that is one more time you have to masturbate on Sunday."

Once again, the masturbation was defined as a punishment, an ordeal, that must be done even more often if the boy did something childish like sucking his thumb. In the interview, the therapist had the young man once again go through the routine of pretending to take off his clothes and fold them neatly and masturbate properly. Again the boy clearly found this to be tedious.

The following week, at the fifth interview, the sister Barbara, instead of the mother, brought the boy to the clinic. Although the therapist had been requesting that the sister come, this was her first appearance. She was a short, obese girl who seemed concerned about her brother. The therapist talked with her for a while, beginning to establish a relationship. After that he saw the boy alone and learned that George had not done his task.

"Do you have the paper for me?" the therapist asked.

"I was outside and forgot it," said George. "I didn't go back upstairs."

"You forgot to bring it?"

"I forgot to take it outside with me."

"Well, did you do what I asked?"

"Uh-huh. I remember how you said to do it, too."

"How many times were you supposed to do it?"

"Twelve."

"How many times did you do it?"

"Six."

"You did it six times?" said the therapist.

"Uh-huh."

"Why didn't you do it all the times I told you?" the therapist said, getting angry. "Why did you let me down? And what did I tell you about your thumbsucking?"

"Every time I suck my thumb, that counts for masturbating."

"Right. You didn't do that either, did you?"

"Huh-uh," said the boy, looking away uneasily.

"Why? I want you to tell me why, now," the therapist said. "I mean it's not fair, it's really not fair. It's not. And you forgot the paper on top of that."

It was important in this procedure for the therapist to condemn the boy for not masturbating as agreed. A confrontation of this kind is the opposite of the one the boy was accustomed to, in which people were angrily condemning him for masturbating. Sometimes it's difficult for a therapist to carry out this condemnation, because he's pleased that the problem is improving. But to accept the improvement and compliment the boy would be an error. Even though the boy came in so cheerfully, looking more mature, and is masturbating less and is more interested in other things, still the condemnation must occur to complete the change.

"Now what did you tell me before you left last week?" asked the therapist.

"I was gonna bring the paper."

"And you was gonna do it, too, right?"

"Uh-huh."

"How do you think that makes me feel?"

"Bad."

"How do you feel? For not doing it? Well, then, why didn't you do it?" The boy looked away. "George, look at me, I'm talking to you. Look at me. Well, I'll tell you what, I don't know, George, I really don't. I don't know if I should trust you anymore. Could I trust you?"

"Uh-huh," said George, beginning to cry.

"You think so?"

"Uh-huh."

"Now, this time," the therapist said, getting up angrily and going to his briefcase to take out some paper, "I'm gonna tell you straight out—now, I don't want no excuses, hear? None at all, right? Because you know what I'm telling you. I could understand if you were a little kid that didn't understand, but you understand, don't you?"

"Uh-huh," said George.

"All right, now come on over here and wipe your eyes." He tossed him a handkerchief casually. "Now this time it's gonna be different because you messed up." The therapist tried to write and the pen wouldn't work, so he angrily threw it into the wastebasket. "My pen doesn't even write, I'm so disgusted with you." He took up another pen and sat beside the boy to write. "Now this is Monday, right?"

"Uh-huh."

"Now, because you didn't do it the way I asked you to do it, I want you to do it Monday one time, in the living room! You understand? In the living room when your mother and sister are there, you understand? Just one time, all right. Tuesday, I want you to do it one time, in the living room. Wednesday, I want you to do it one time, in the living room. Thursday, I want you to do it one time, in the living room. Friday, one time, in the living room. Right? Saturday, one time, in the living room, you understand?"

"Uh-huh," said George.

"On Sunday, I want you to do it *eight* times, right? Now how many times did I say to do it?"

"Eight on Sunday."

"Eight. Now I'm gonna write it here because you might forget again, and I'm not going for that no more. Now when you suck your thumb, you got to do it one more time on Sunday. You understand?"

"Uh-huh."

"I don't want no excuses when you come back, hear? Now here's another thing. I won't see you next Wednesday."

"Uh-huh."

"But I'll see you the following Wednesday. Right?"

"Uh-huh."

"All right?" The therapist repeated that he wanted the boy to do it as it said on the paper for one week, but he wouldn't see him for two weeks. "You understand now?" he said. "You're supposed to do it once a day where?"

"In the living room."

"Right, and on Sunday—how many times?"

"Eight."

"Now don't forget the paper, hear? Go ahead," he said, gesturing for the boy to sign the paper. Then he sighed, saying, "Let me sign this again. I hate to be signing my name to things and you don't do it." He added at the end, "But we're still buddies, okay? Here, wipe your eyes now."

Although it sounds severe to tell the boy he must masturbate in front of his family in the living room, still that is only asking him to do what he is doing anyhow. It has taken five weeks for the therapist to arrange that the boy's ordeal is to do exactly what he was doing as a presenting problem.

The purpose in instructing the boy in his punishment for one week and not seeing him in two weeks is to leave open what the boy might do the second week. He is without instructions for that week. Allowing a week without a task allows the therapist to see how much spontaneous change will take place. The goal isn't to have the boy do what he is told but, rather, to "spontaneously" behave more normally. If the boy drops the public masturbation the second week, the issue of masturbation can be dropped. If he continues his old pattern unchanged, the therapist can continue the ordeal until some future time and then let up to see whether the change will continue without instruction.

At the sixth interview, two weeks later, the therapist saw the boy and mother together and learned that the boy was becoming less passive.

"We have to get him back on the ball again," said the mother. "I had to go to school for him. The teacher says he won't listen."

"He won't listen?" asked the therapist.

"Yeah. And he starts playing around in the room instead of doing his work like he used to. There is another boy in his room that she says he has been following behind. So he's gonna get back on the ball again in school or else get a whipping."

It was unusual for this boy to play or make trouble in the class, and the therapist, surprised, inquired further about it.

"The teacher sent for me," the mother said. "Because she said he had changed and she knew he could do better."

"She said he had changed?"

"Uh-huh, she knew he could do better. He had started to play around quite a bit in the room."

"Well," the therapist said, "Im sure you will remember what I discussed with you about being able to accept a change. I also said I didn't think you could accept it."

"I haven't spanked him yet," said the mother, "but George can do better work than he is doing."

The boy appeared more mature in his appearance and

clothes. Alone with him later in the interview, the therapist tried to determine what had happened during the two-week absence. Determining what had happened was not a simple matter, particularly when the boy brought in the wrong chart, with a whole variety of numbers distributed randomly on it.

"What did you do here?" asked the therapist.

"I had to do it eight times on Sunday. You mean up here?"

"Uh-huh."

"I just put them numbers there."

"Mmm," the therapist said in a friendly way. "You just wrote those in there?"

"I like to write the numbers," said George.

"Well, what happened the following week? This week that just passed?"

"I don't know."

It seemed to the therapist that the boy had amnesia for that second week. "Just what did you do?" he asked again.

"Well, I was doing my homework, my written homework."

"Did you do any masturbating?"

"Yeah."

"When?"

"I don't remember what day it was."

"You don't remember."

"I think I was doing some Monday. I don't know."

"You're not sure. Well, you been pretty good, you know that? You been doing a good job. And I've been kind of hard on you, haven't I?"

"No."

"I haven't?"

"No."

"You don't think so?"

"Not to me."

"Good. I think I've been kind of rough on you, though. I'm gonna give you a break. Okay. I'm not gonna tell you to do it like I said, you know?"

"Yeah."

"I guess for a while we're just gonna forget about it. Okay?"

"Right."

"I ain't gonna give you any more papers. We'll just, you know, just forget about it for a little while, for about a week or two. Okay?"

"Uh-huh."

"Then you'll have more time to go out and play. You won't have to be writing things down. Okay?"

"Uh-huh."

"Let's forget about it for a little while. Talk about some of the things you like."

"I'm going to camp," the boy said quickly, obviously relieved to drop the subject of masturbation.

"You are? When?"

"I don't know what day, but I'm going to Mountain Camp."

"You are? That's good. Who got you into camp?"

"The school. I'm gonna stay for two weeks."

"Oh, that's good," the therapist said, "That's real good." He was impressed because this was the first time the mother had allowed the boy to go somewhere overnight, far less to go away for two weeks.

It was decided to drop the subject of masturbation to see whether the boy continued to improve without focusing on the problem. During this period the therapist dealt with mother and daughter, Barbara, over their struggles with each other. The boy was present in the interviews. The therapeutic goals were to have the daughter lose weight and to take care of her children responsibly and move out of the house into a place of her own with her boyfriend, which both mother and daughter wanted. It was also a goal to have mother drink less and begin to get involved in school or work so that she had more in her life than just her struggle with her children. Mother joined AA and also began looking for a job. The therapist wished to check on the relationship with the son to be sure that mother did not shift back to the son as she disengaged from the daughter. He saw the mother alone and asked her about the current situation with the masturbation.

"When he's not outside," the mother said, "he just can't sit down and look at television or do something without that thumb in the mouth and the other hand—" she gestured toward her lap, "and it looks like lately he's been doing it a little more openly, you know."

"Mm-hm," said the therapist.

"And I sit there and watch him, you know. I don't say nothing. I just sit there and watch him—a couple of times I said something to him."

The therapist was puzzled by the mother's description. He asked, "What would he be doing? Would his hands be still, or would he be moving or motionless or what?"

"Not too much movement," said the mother.

As she described the boy's actions, it seemed that he just put his thumb in his belt or in his zipper. As she said, "He had like his thumb, just his thumb was in the zipper, but then he knew I was watching, you know."

The problem did not seem to be masturbation but a game between mother and son. He would put his thumb in his belt or his zipper until she told him not to. It was decided not to focus on the activity but to deal with other problems on the assumption that this issue would disappear as mother's other problems were solved. The therapy continued to focus on the daughter. Two months later the therapist did a follow-up interview with the mother and boy to see how the masturbation problem was. When asked whether the problem was better, the mother said, "Oh, yes. Because when we first started, sometimes I would get up during the night and check in his room. He would have his hands in his shorts. You know?"

"Mm-hm," said the therapist. "So that's not happening now?"

"Not that I noticed," the mother said.

The therapist asked about the thumbsucking, and the mother reported that it was occasional.

When the boy was asked about the masturbation problem, he said it was over. As the mother put it, "I think George can tell you better than I can. I haven't noticed him doing it. Have you been sticking your hands inside your pants?"

"No," the boy said.

The therapy continued intermittently, focusing on the

problems of mother and daughter. The masturbation symptom, which had been a problem for five years, had been resolved in eight interviews over a period of ten weeks.

There was a five-year follow-up to determine how the change had persisted over the years. The daughter, Barbara, was living with her husband. George was fifteen years old and was doing well in school. The mother reported that the public masturbation problem had ended during the therapy and never resumed. George was seen alone in a carefully planned interview to try to determine whether he now masturbated privately and whether it gave him pleasure. Despite the interviewer's skill, the boy would not say whether he masturbated or not. The presenting problem had been public masturbation. At this point, the masturbation was so private that it could not be determined whether it was happening.

9

————————————————————

What About the Schoolteacher?

When asked to choose his most important single problem, the man said he would like to have sexual relations with a woman. He was thirty-four years old, tall, nice-looking, educated, with a good income. Somehow he had never succeeded in getting into bed with a woman, no matter how he wished for it. Occasionally he had social engagements with women, but he could not make the step from being an acquaintance to being intimate. Years before, when in his teens, he had had "a sort of a sexual experience" with a prostitute in Paris, but he had never been romantically involved.

The man—we shall call him the Doctor of Mathematics—was asked to choose a single problem because I saw no point in doing a generalized therapy with a man who had already had so many years of therapy. He had been through psychoanalysis twice with two different analysts, and after those years he had

gone to a behavior modifier to reduce his anxieties. Less anxious after the behavior therapy, he was still discontented with
his life.

I said I would take the man on in therapy only if there
was a particular problem he wanted changed. He decided the
sexual problem was worthy of therapy. It was also a challenge,
since he had been successful in avoiding sex for many years.
The therapeutic problem was increased because sex had to be
with the right sort of woman. A proper and conservative man,
the good Doctor did not wish to seek out "women of the evening" but wanted a relationship with a woman he could associate with socially. His primary experience with women had
been with his mother. An only child, he had been the only
company for his mother after his father died. Finally she married again, and that enabled the Doctor to leave home and
establish himself in another state. He was extremely shy in social situations and had almost no friends.

Talking to the Doctor of Mathematics to find what resources might exist in his life to solve this problem, I found the
situation a difficult one. The man lived a lonely life not only
because of his interests but because of the nature of his work.
He was a mathematician, sufficiently exceptional in that field
to be a one-man department in a "think tank." He was paid to
think about whatever he wished, or research any problem he
chose, on the assumption that whatever he did would ultimately
be valuable. Being a one-man department limited his opportu-
nities for social exchanges with other people. In fact, he usually worked at home in his apartment, since there was no one in
his office to supervise him or associate with him. This meant that
his days were largely spent alone.

Looking for possible candidates for a sexual adventure, I
asked what women were available. The man's evenings were almost, but not quite, as lonely as his days. He belonged to no
social groups or clubs and had no close friends. He hardly had
acquaintances. However, there were two women he occasionally
took out to dinner or a concert. One of them seemed more of a
possibility than the other.

The one who did not seem to be a candidate who would

spring into bed easily was a scientist, a biologist. Though in her thirties, she had hardly ever dated, having been devoted to scientific endeavors. The man described her as plump, a bit plain, and more pleasant as an intelligent colleague than as a sex object. She had two Ph.D.s and was in a high rank in academia, so they shared scientific interests. However, there was no romantic involvement. Their social engagements usually consisted of an evening at the symphony and a formal goodnight handshake.

Dismissing the biologist as a likely candidate, I asked about the other woman in his life. She was described as a schoolteacher in her twenties, a carefree woman, single and living in an apartment by herself. "She has a sense of humor," said the Doctor. "For example, she has her bedroom decorated like a pirate's den." When I asked how he knew what her bedroom looked like, he said that once when he'd picked her up for a date, she'd given him a tour of her bedroom to show him the decor. He added that she was also careless about leaving her bedroom door open while he was waiting in the living room. "Sometimes while she's dressing she walks back and forth in front of the open door with very little on. She's so casual, she doesn't notice something like that."

Asking more about this casual female, I learned that she had even sat on the Doctor's lap at a party. "That was only because there were no chairs available," he said.

The Doctor had taken the schoolteacher out several times, but he didn't think she cared much for him. As he described incidents with her, I thought otherwise, suspecting the woman was trying to entice the Doctor into a more romantic involvement. She seemed a likely prospect for achieving the therapeutic goal.

The task of the therapy seemed to be to encourage, or force, the good Doctor to take the step from a friendly involvement with a female to a romantic involvement that included sex. Accepting the problem, I put a condition on the therapy. I was concerned because the Doctor of Mathematics seemed to hint that he had the old-fashioned idea that if a gentleman has sexual relations with a woman, he should marry her. Concerned about the man's loneliness, I said, "I want you to agree not to rush into marriage with a woman just because you had sexual relations with her."

"I'll agree to that," he said.

"I think you should get to know a dozen women well before you choose one to marry," I said, "and not get married immediately to the first woman who shows you intimate affection. Let me put it more strongly," I emphasized. "I want you to give me your word that you won't get married while you are having therapy with me unless I give you permission."

"I agree," said the man, "since I'm certainly not in a hurry to marry."

Although I was concerned about the man's getting married precipitously, there was another purpose in asking him not to marry immediately after getting over the problem. Putting it like that is a way of getting the man to accept the idea that he will get over the problem. To agree to do (or not do) something after an event means accepting the idea that the event will happen. The man was more likely to have sexual relations if he believed it would happen and was inevitable.

In the first two interviews I talked with the man about his life and about women while seeking some way to gain the leverage that would encourage the man to get into bed with a woman and so achieve his goal. The man was so abstract in his thinking, so withdrawn and shy in his social behavior, that it began to be apparent that simple encouragement, or education about himself and women, would not achieve the goal.

As I talked to the Doctor about what he should do more, the man appeared to do everything that a man his age should, except have a sex life. He exercised regularly, wrote dutifully to his mother, and generally fulfilled a citizen's obligations. The only thing he could think of that he should do more of was read scientific papers. He said that in his apartment there were stacks of scientific journals that he simply had not taken the time to read. He should do so if he was to keep up on the various technical fields his work involved.

At the end of the second interview, I was ready. I said, "I can solve this problem and guarantee you will have sexual relations with a woman, but you have to agree to do exactly what I say."

"No matter what?"

"No matter what."

The Doctor of Mathematics began to look excited at the prospect and said he was willing to do anything. I said he had not thought about it enough yet. He should come back the following week only if he was sure he was willing to do anything asked of him. I said that what I had in mind was something that was not criminal, that it would not harm him and in fact would be good for him, and it was something he would be able to do.

The following week the Doctor came in vowing he would do what I asked. "I want to go to bed with a woman," he said, "and so I am willing to do anything."

"Fine," I said. "What I'll ask of you will not begin for thirty days." I wished to give the man an opportunity to solve the problem himself so an ordeal would not be necessary.

The Doctor was disappointed. "I'm ready right now," he said.

"This is the first of September," I said. "What I'm asking you to do will begin on October 1. If, before that time, you have sexual relations with a woman, of course you don't have to do what I ask."

"All right, what do I do?"

"On the night of October 1," I said, looking at the desk calendar, "which is a Friday, you have to set your alarm clock for two o'clock in the morning."

"What do I do at two in the morning?"

"I don't want you to stay awake until two o'clock. I want you to go to sleep and have the alarm clock wake you up."

"All right," said the man.

"When you get up," I went on, "I want you to take your unread stack of scientific journals and read them for one hour. Since you might doze off to sleep if you sat down or lay down while reading, I want you to stand up and read for that hour."

"Stand up and read a journal?" The Doctor looked at me, astonished. "At two in the morning?"

"You are to finish at three o'clock, even if the reading is

interesting, and go back to bed and to sleep. It's important that you go back to sleep so that this episode in the night is like a dream."

"That's it?" asked the Doctor.

"On October 2, the following night," I went on, "if you have not had sexual relations with a woman, you have to set your alarm for two o'clock in the morning. Once again you are to get up and read scientific journals while standing for one hour. Then go back to sleep."

"And the next night?"

"Every night, until you have sexual relations, you have to follow this procedure," I said. "The task ends when you have sexual relations with a woman or you are eighty years old, whichever comes first."

"Good God," said the man, dismayed.

"It isn't all that difficult. You wanted to get to the journals anyhow."

"Reading standing up at two in the morning?" said the Doctor.

"I know it's hard," I said. "Personally I like to sleep comfortably through the night." I changed the subject, and we talked about other matters in the man's life. He seemed preoccupied. At the end of the interview, he said, "I'm going to arrange a date for tonight."

"No hurry," I said. "Take your time and think about it. You have thirty days."

"Maybe tonight isn't possible, but I'll arrange one by tomorrow night," he said, and he left.

The following week the Doctor came in and told an amazing story. He was both pleased with himself and frustrated at his lack of success. "I left here and went and telephoned the woman biologist," he said. "She was free that night, so we went to a piano recital. Afterwards I took her home. I tried to kiss her goodnight at the door. She held me off and said, 'No, we shouldn't.' So I left, and I called her and asked her to dinner the following night."

"Why the biologist?" I asked. "What about the schoolteacher?"

"No, I decided I would make love to the biologist," said

the Doctor. "So I arranged to have dinner with her at my apartment." He described how he had arranged a candlelight dinner, with music and a good wine. "She came, and she looked much more attractive than usual."

"So what happened?"

"I made a pass at her," he said. He described how after dinner he had taken her to the couch and put his arms around her. She pulled away, and he tried to pull her back. She stood up, and he tried to pull her back down onto the couch. She ran from the room, saying, "What kind of a woman do you think I am?"

"She really said that?" I asked. "I didn't think anyone said that anymore."

"She said that," said the man. He described how she had run out of the house and down the street to her car. He ran after her. He sat down in the car with her and apologized for his gauche behavior. She stopped weeping and said that she hadn't realized what a forceful and aggressive man he was. He said he hadn't realized what a sexually attractive woman she was.

"So what happened?" I asked.

"I blew it again," said the Doctor. "I started putting my arms around her and kissing her. She got all upset and cried and ordered me out of the car. She went home. The next day I sent her flowers and apologized and did what I could to make it up. What an ass I made of myself!"

"Why the hurry?" I said. "You have until the first of October, which is three weeks away. Why rush after the woman?"

"I don't know," said the Doctor. "I just couldn't help myself. I had this determination."

"What about the schoolteacher? If you approached her in the same way, you might be surprised at what would happen."

"Maybe so," said the man, but he didn't sound interested. He was mostly contrite over the way he had treated the biologist. As the interview was ending, I suggested that the man have a less adventurous week and we would talk the matter over more the following week.

"All right," said the Doctor. As he rose to leave, he said, "Oh, I almost forgot. I have to go to Philadelphia to a meeting, and so I'll have to miss our appointment next week."

"All right," I said, "we'll meet at the same time in two weeks."

"Fine," said the Doctor. He went to the door and turned, saying casually that the biologist had forgiven him. In fact, she just happened to need to go to Philadelphia herself that week, and so they were driving together.

"She just happened to be going?" I asked.

"Yes," said the Doctor. "Isn't that a coincidence." And he went out the door.

I sat in dismay, almost calling the man back. Having a premonition of misfortune, I didn't believe it was a coincidence that the biologist was traveling with him. Nor did I believe that her resistance to his advances was only maidenly modesty. But I decided we could deal with the matter when he returned.

Two weeks later the Doctor of Mathematics came in and sat down. He sighed and said, "I'm getting married tomorrow."

"What!" I said. "That's not possible!"

"I can hardly believe it myself," he said.

"You can't get married tomorrow. Who are you marrying?" I asked, as if I didn't know.

The man said he was marrying the biologist. Her family and his mother were on the way and were expected to arrive that night. All of them were coming to the marriage ceremony.

"You promised," I said. "You gave me your word that you would not get married without my permission."

The Doctor looked contrite. "I know," he said. "I meant to keep that promise, too." He sighed, "I don't quite know what happened."

"Do you want to get married?"

"No—well, yes—I don't know," said the man. "It doesn't matter anyhow, because I have to. It's all arranged. It's like I'm on a train that can only go down the tracks to that destination."

"Tell me what happened."

The Doctor said that he and the woman biologist had gone to Philadelphia. She was going to stay with friends, and he was going to stay in the hotel where his scientific meeting was being held. Before he went to the hotel, they sat together in the park on a bench. It was a lovely day, and the two of them had enjoyed the ride together and the conversation. In the park they chatted affectionately. At a certain point, he put an arm around her. She didn't pull away. He kissed her on the cheek. She kissed him back. "So then," he said, "I blew it again. I said, 'Let's go to my hotel room.' I was determined to get to bed with her. She was devastated by my suggestion." He sighed. "She began to weep, and I apologized. She said she would not go to bed with a man unless she was married to him because she was that kind of woman. I said, 'Will you marry me?' She said, 'Yes, let's call your mother and my parents and tell them we're getting married.'" The Doctor gestured vaguely. "It was something like that. I'm not sure what happened. Before I knew it we were at a public phone telling my mother that we were getting married and we would have the ceremony this Saturday. She called her mother, who was so pleased."

"Just like that."

"Yes, just like that," the Doctor said. "She didn't come to my hotel room, because she wants to wait until we're married."

"Of course."

We talked awhile, and the Doctor went on his way. The next week he called and said, "I don't have to get up in the night and read those papers like you said. And it's not even October 1 yet."

"So the problem is solved."

"Yes," said the Doctor. His tone was neither pleased nor displeased.

When I hung up the telephone, I could not decide whether the case was a failure or a success.

10

❖━━❖━━❖━━❖━━❖━━❖━━❖━━❖━━❖━━❖

I Want My
Rubber Band

The eight-year-old boy, Arthur, looked like an angel. He was slim and blond. His hair was carefully combed. He sat with his hands folded in his lap. According to the report, he had hit his teacher, who was twice his size and weight, so hard he had broken her nose and put her in the hospital with a concussion. Arthur was from a pleasant, middle-class family. His father, also named Arthur, was a tall young man wearing horn-rimmed glasses. His mother was a blond, nervous-looking woman. At the first interview his six-year-old sister, Ruthie, was also present.

The therapist facing this problem—Marcha Ortiz, a psychiatric nurse—said to the parents, "From what was told me over the telephone, I understand you're here because of trouble at school."

"That's what brought us here," the father said, "but there are other problems." He spoke slowly and uncertainly, as if uneasy about talking to a therapist.

"Tell me about it," said Mrs. Ortiz.

"We're mainly concerned about Arthur having trouble controlling his temper," the father said. "When he gets into a situation where he doesn't get his way, he immediately goes into a tantrum. It seems to be uncontrollable and really upsets the house. These aren't just normal little fits. They're just bad. I have no control over what happens."

As the father talked, the mother sat listening nervously. The little girl put out her tongue at her brother, who looked away from her.

"Is the problem at home or in school?" asked the therapist.

"It's school *and* home. It just recently flared up at home. The problems started at school about three years ago when there were one or two small incidents."

"What happened?"

"Well," the father said, "I don't mean to nail Arthur down as the problem, because it isn't really just him, it's everybody. We're just using you as a case study," he said to Arthur. "The problem is with everybody, really."

"I know I have a temper," the little boy said.

"I'll get everyone's ideas as we go," said the therapist, turning back to the father.

"The problems go way back," the father said, "but as far as school, well, I never got the complete story, but an incident occurred and Arthur turned around and hit the teacher and broke her nose. That was traumatic for us."

"With a ruler, or . . . ?" the therapist asked, impressed with the small size of the boy.

"With his fist. Clobbered her right in the nose. After that we had a session with the teacher and principal, and Arthur eventually apologized to the teacher. But I feel like he never really felt any sorrow for the situation. Maybe that is beside the point. Since that incident, we have been managing, except Arthur doesn't like to do any schoolwork. He just freaks out if he's asked to do it. Anyhow after that incident my wife and I had eight weeks of Parent Effectiveness Training. I've tried to use it. My wife says I don't try, but I do. Sometimes it's effec-

tive, and other times it doesn't deal with the situation, especially the tantrums. So about a month ago we got a book from a
neighbor who has a hyperactive child. We decided the problem
might be Arthur's diet. So we put him on the diet, but he fell
off it occasionally. Since he has been on a diet, at least once a
day he has a flare-up. He hasn't been able to control his tantrums at all."

The mother, when asked about the problem, said, "It's
been coming on slowly for years. It's been building up. In kin-
dergarten and first and second grade he had really excellent
teachers. Really understanding people. But at times he just
balks and refuses to do what he is asked. When he gets it into
his head not to do something, he doesn't do it. Nothing will
move him. The problem is coming to a head now. Because when
he goes—we never know when he's going to go. After it's over,
he's exhausted and half the time crying. He hit his teacher so
hard she was hospitalized overnight. He really hurt her. She had
two black eyes and a concussion. Now he's in another classroom, and he's very unhappy."

When asked to discuss the situation further, the mother
said, "He has to control everything. He has to be in control. If
he loses control of the situation, he seems to feel he's losing his
grip and he has to be the boss. He has to tell the teacher what
he will do and what he won't do. Now he's ostracized in the
classroom."

The therapist asked the boy about the situation. He said,
"I think I'm doing better in the classroom I'm in right now. I
think if I try, I can get better grades and stuff. I want to stay on
the diet, but I keep falling off of it."

"What's hardest for you?" the therapist asked.

"My temper tantrums. My dad got me a punching bag,
and when I'm not having a temper tantrum, I punch around on
it, and that sort of helps. I usually have a lot of energy when I
have my temper tantrums."

"Okay," the therapist said, "now I just want to talk to
your parents for a few minutes, so I'll show you young people
to the waiting room."

Alone with the parents, the therapist said, "I just wanted

to talk to you alone about what has worked in the past when raising this young man, and your daughter." She asked how the six-year-old dealt with her brother.

"Ruthie fights him now," the father said. "She used to be afraid of him, but now she's standing up to him. He'll slug her and she'll stand there and and take it. In a way it's good, but in another way I'm afraid she'll get her head knocked off."

"Are you afraid of this boy?" asked the therapist.

"I'll tell you," the father said, admiration in his voice, "we had an unbelievable incident about a week ago. I've heard about all his tantrums, but he's never really had one in front of me. About two weeks ago he was being stubborn about something and he had one. I grabbed a paddle and spanked him on the fanny. It was breaking my heart to do that. And it didn't do a thing. It doesn't matter what you do, it doesn't faze him. He would never show if it fazed him."

"That didn't get the change you wanted?" said the therapist.

"No, he just started slugging me. I let him do it, and he just stood there and hit me as hard as he could."

The therapist reviewed what they had tried: the diet, the Parent Effectiveness Training, and spanking.

The mother said, "This tantrum behavior is a specific, separate thing. It's almost as if a switch is thrown inside him."

"Are you afraid of this boy?" the therapist asked the mother.

"I'm not afraid of him on a personal level," said the mother. "But I watch him carefully. I don't want him to hurt himself, or to hurt another person, or to wreck the house." She laughed. "So I mean I'm not personally afraid he's going to injure me. But it's very unpleasant."

"What scares me is, I don't understand it," the father said. "It's not normal."

"Yeah, it's certainly not normal," said the mother.

"I've never seen a kid get mad like this before. It's really scary, because it's just like—he's possessed. I've even thought of that. He's just another person."

"He seems to have this tremendous anger," the mother

said, "and I want to know what's beneath the anger. What's his motivation? He's very insecure. Many, many times he's said, 'Daddy doesn't love me. I know Daddy really hates me.' And mostly I just let him talk, and when he gets it out, I'll give him specific instances of what his father has done for him."

After learning that the couple's families of origin weren't in that area and so there were no grandparents or aunts and uncles to help them, the therapist brought the boy back into the room, leaving his sister playing in the waiting room.

Asking for a specific incident that had been a problem at school, the therapist learned there had been one that week. "It had to do with a rubber band," said the mother. The therapist asked the boy to describe what happened.

"My teacher sent me to the office," the boy said, "because you're not allowed to have your hands like this, or something." He showed a wiggling of hands that the teacher apparently objected to. "She sent me to the office, and right outside the door I picked up a rubber band. I was sort of fiddling around with it. I got to the office, and someone was already sitting in the chair that I usually sit on." (He was in the principal's office so often that he had his special chair.) "So I took another chair and moved up so that I had a sort of a desk place. I was fiddling around with my rubber band, and one of the kids from my class came up and gave me some work to do. I was looking at the book, and the secretary came up and took the rubber band away from me. She said, 'If you don't finish the work, I won't give you the rubber band back.' I wanted her to give me the rubber band back, so I went over to get it and she pushed me away. That's what started it."

"That's what started what?" asked the therapist. "What happened then?"

"Well, I can't remember all of it," said the boy vaguely.

When the therapist asked the parents to find out more clearly what the objectionable behavior at school had been, the father began to interrogate the boy about what had happened. He asked what had started the whole thing in the first place. The boy said, "The rubber band." The father said it seemed to have started in the classroom and asked what had happened there. Describing a substitute teacher that day, the boy said, "She told me to sit down quietly. I stopped fiddling my fingers, but she said I still wasn't sitting down quietly. So she sent me to the office. Outside the door I picked up the rubber band."

"When you were fiddling with your fingers," said the father, "after she asked you to stop it, did you keep doing it?"

"After the first time I stopped, and the second time I had to go to the office. I didn't do it, but I don't know what happened. She is a weird substitute teacher, and I never did like her."

The father asked about the rubber band incident, and the therapist handed him a rubber band to give to the boy to act out what had happened. The boy showed how he'd been playing with the rubber band when the secretary took it. "Did she say, 'Give it to me,' or what?" the father asked.

"She said, 'Give it to me.' "

"And you gave it to her?"

"Yes," said the boy. "I said, 'What are you going to do with it?' She said, 'I'm not going to give it back to you until you finish the work.' "

"And that made you mad?" the father asked.

"Yeah, because I was trying to finish the work. I told her that, and she said, 'I'm sorry, finish the work first and I'll give you the rubber band.' I said to her, 'I don't know what to do. If you'll tell me what to do, I'll do it. But you have to give me the rubber band back.' That's what started it. Because then I went over to get the rubber band, and she pushed me away."

"Okay, show me," said the father, and the boy showed how he had walked over to get the rubber band. "What did she say?" asked the father.

"She said, 'Do your work, Arthur.' I said, 'First I want the rubber band.' Because I was trying to find out what to do for work. Then she started arguing with me and trying to get me to sit down, because I wanted the rubber band."

"She ordered you to sit down?" the father asked.

"Yeah, she was ordering me around and stuff. Then Mrs. Jones called up home, and that's when I went home."

"Did you start screaming obscenities at her?"

"I said, 'Lay off me.' "

"Did she push you?"

"Yeah, she was pushing me all over the place."

"Like this?" the father asked, pushing him to illustrate.

"Yeah," said Arthur, "I was afraid she was going to make me back out the window or something."

The mother spoke up and said, "Well, you were crying, too. When I got there, you were really crying."

"No," said the boy. "I wasn't crying, but they pushed me. Three people were pushing me down, and I couldn't move."

"Who were the three people?" the mother asked.

"Two secretaries, and the man from the retarded class. He was pushing me down, too."

"Were you fighting back?" asked the father.

"Yeah, I was trying to get up."

"Were you trying to hit them? The secretary said you hit her on the arm, right?"

"Yeah, but not very hard. Because they were pushing me around like heck. I hit her because she was the person pushing me. I got her to the wall, and then Miss Doughty said, 'If we leave you alone, will you stop?' I said, 'Yeah, if you leave me alone, I will.' And I stopped, and that's when you came in," he said to the mother.

The therapist asked the mother, "Would you pick up from when you came in?"

"I had no idea what was going on," the mother said. "The secretary called me. She's a mild-mannered, very quiet person. I've known her about four years, and she has always been a good friend to us. She called, and she was really shaky on the phone. She said, 'Can you please come right down, we need you.' Right away I turned to jelly inside. I thought maybe he fell off the jungle gym and fractured his skull or something. I had no idea what had happened. So when I walked in, he was standing sort of against the wall and was very shaky. Both the secretaries were nervous wrecks and looking like they were going to cry. Arthur was crying, and I went up to him right away."

"I wasn't crying," said Arthur. "I just couldn't get my breath. They were pushing me into the wall."

The mother went on, "I said, 'Arthur, what happened?'

and all he would say was 'I want my rubber band.' I asked him what happened, and he just said again, 'I want my rubber band.' I could tell he had been hysterical. So finally one of the secretaries pulled out a rubber band and said, 'There was a problem over this.' I took the thing and handed him the rubber band. I said, 'Come on, we're going home.' I could tell there was no way he was going to go back to the classroom that day. The secretaries were a nervous wreck, and he was, too. So I just removed him."

When asked how the father had been told about it, the mother said she had telephoned him. "I don't usually call during the day with bad news," she said, "but I figured he'd better know what was going on. When he got home, I talked with him about it. This was after the incident with the broken nose, and he had been screaming profanities in the office and had hit the secretary. I didn't know if he could go back to the school or not. I was really upset."

"And what did you do with the young man?" the therapist asked the father.

"I talked to him to find out exactly what happened. I don't know. I began to realize that we really do need help bad. Before the problem was of this magnitude, I used to think maybe—"

The boy interrupted, saying, "Well, let me just tell you—"

"Your daddy is talking now," said the therapist.

The father continued, "I used to think he didn't get enough attention from me, or something. I was on a guilt trip. So I went out of my way to do things with him. It just didn't make any difference."

"Well, that helped," the boy said.

"Sure, it helped," said the father, rather sadly.

"So you tried talking, and you tried spending more time with him," the therapist said. "What other things have you tried? You see, there is no sense in us making a plan for something that you have already done and it wasn't effective."

"Well," the father said, "I feel we're desperate. We don't know what to do now. The last thing is, my wife and I knelt down and were praying last week."

"Okay, so you tried praying. What else did you try in the past?"

"The Parent Effectiveness Training."

"The diet," said the mother.

"Yeah," the father said, "the diet, and the praying we're going to do more of."

"Yes," the mother said. "I was going to say that, too. My pediatrician is very old-fashioned, too. He said, 'Don't spank with your hand. If you're going to spank, go to the dime store and get a flat paddle. It stings and it doesn't do any damage.' I did that, and I found—well, as far as I'm concerned, I think that was a big mistake. It was wrong."

"So you tried a paddle."

"And spanking. But I never want to go back to that."

When asked by the therapist whom the boy would hit, the father said that his tantrums could occur with anybody. "Sometimes he'll get so frustrated he'll pick up the whole dining room table—which is heavy. He's strong as an ox. He'll just pick it up and let it drop. The night he had the tantrum with me, I told him, 'Wreck the house, I don't care.' I was fed up. He started throwing things and breaking things up, and finally I had to tell him to stop."

"When he hits his sister, Ruthie," the therapist asked, "what is the consequence for that? What can he expect to have happen if he hits someone like that?"

There was a long pause, and it was evident that no clear consequence was involved. "I don't know," said the father. "It depends on the situation. Usually I just get mad. I have my own little tantrum. Which is probably where he picks them up. I don't know." He gestured helplessly.

"So if you're around, he can expect that he'll get a rise out of you, and you might have your own tantrum."

"Well, lately I've been trying this Parent Effectiveness stuff. If he hits his sister, I'll put them apart. If I know she's in the right, then I'll give him equal hits with a paddle, or with my hand. But it means absolutely nothing. It's out of frustration that I do it."

"When the hitting starts," the mother said, "I'm worried

about Ruthie. Sometimes she eggs him on because she knows that if she gets hit, she gets a lot of sympathy. So she asks for it. She'll pick at him, because her way is to pick and nag, and his way is to hit. He's very aggressive and she's more picky."

"It's a blueprint of us," the father said, gesturing to himself and his wife.

"You don't go around hitting me," laughed the wife.

"How does that go?" the therapist asked.

"I used to have the same kind of tantrums that Arthur has," said the father. "I didn't get as violent. I didn't lose control."

"You didn't hit me," the wife said, "but you got pretty wild."

"For the first five years of our marriage, I used to go bananas," the father said. "She used to frustrate me to death. I had no way to vent my frustrations, so I just screamed and yelled. I would be so frustrated, I just wanted to bang my head against the wall. Just like Arthur gets, just terribly frustrated."

"I do it, but I don't want to," said Arthur.

"He gets very frustrated," the father said. "But if I hit my wife, I'd kill her. One time I slapped her, and I heard about it for years after that. I've calmed myself down the last two or three years. I've gained control, and I'm more settled in my marriage. We understand each other better. Not that we don't have fights—we do. But somehow I'm better able to control, and I feel for Arthur because he has no control over this situation."

At this point the therapist had the information she needed. She consulted with the supervisor, and a plan of action was devised. The problem was not simply to decide what to suggest to the parents but to choose something the parents would carry out. At that moment they felt helpless and thought they had done everything that could be done. Motivating them to act and do something was as important as deciding what they might do to prevent future violence by their son. The problem was not to educate them, since they knew what they should do and even how to do it, but to get them to do it.

The therapist presented a simple plan to the parents. Persuading them to carry out the task, which would be an ordeal for them, required preparation and persuasive techniques. First of all, it was assumed that whatever the function of the boy's violence, or whatever its meaning, it indicated that the hierarchy of the family was in confusion. The parents were not in charge of the family; the boy was increasingly in charge. Whenever there was a struggle, the boy determined what happened. It was necessary for the parents to join together and take charge, whatever the division between them, and to do so in a way that gave them an opportunity to succeed.

The first steps had already been taken in persuading the parents to act. The gravity of the problem had been emphasized by interviewing the whole family instead of merely child or mother. During the interview, the children were sent from the room to clarify the generational line between parents and child and to focus on the executive status of the parents.

When parents and therapist had established an atmosphere of joint concern, the problem boy was brought in to face the issue, while his sister was left out. This helped focus the parents on the specific problem.

The therapist did not merely condemn the boy; that would have made the parents feel she was too harsh and didn't understand. Instead, she sympathized with the boy and even complimented him on his intelligence. The parents were thereby allowed to think of the problem they had as different from other parents', and the task of dealing with the son was defined as a challenge.

The problems at school and home were merged together by having child and parents act out what had happened at school in the incident of the rubber band. This was a way of bringing the problem into the room instead of merely having it talked about. Finally, the therapist took the most direct route and simply told the parents they had to get their son under control. Whatever their objections, they had no choice and must act.

"I think this young man is probably one step ahead of you," the therapist said, "if not two. It's going to take both of you putting your heads together with me if we're going to find a way that is going to work." She smiled at the parents. "This is the time now," she said, "to give a child tools for when he gets older. And it's up to the two of you to handle this. You have to. There is just no other way around it. You can think of special schools or other alternatives, but ultimately it comes back to you folks—the ones who matter most to him. You have to take charge of this young man in order to raise him properly. There's no question of abdicating, you just have to do it, that's all. This week we'll develop a plan, and when you come back next week, we'll move on from there. Are you willing to take action to make a change?"

The therapist studied the parents seriously, and they looked at her, puzzled.

"Sure," the father said.

"That's why we're here," said the mother.

Actually, they were not necessarily there to take action to change. Many parents come to talk about a problem or to have an expert comment on their situation or to get some advice. To make a change might not be what they have in mind. That is why the therapist asked these parents for a commitment to do something.

"Okay," said the therapist, "let's get clear what problem is important to you. What I hear most mentioned is the temper tantrums."

"That's number one," the father said.

"That includes swearing or hitting or . . ."

"Or stubbornness," said the mother.

"We can classify all that as temper tantrums," the therapist said. "It sounds like that is the biggest thing."

The parents agreed that the temper tantrums were the main problem, and they agreed they could clearly know whether Arthur was having one or not, so there was no doubt about that.

"What I'm going to ask you to do," the therapist said, "is really rather simple. It is to put him in a room by himself whenever he has a temper tantrum."

The parents looked at the boy and then at each other, clearly in doubt about what such action might achieve.

"We need a spare room. It might or might not be *his*

room," said the therapist. "It could be the bathroom or maybe a sewing area or some other place."

"Well," the mother said, "is this something that will be agreeable to him also?"

"No, he really has no choice about it," the therapist said. "That's what's nice about being parents. They are older and wiser, and they have walked some of the same road before."

"Yes, but the problem is, he is stronger than I am," said the mother.

At this point the therapy centered on the simple instruction to provide the boy with an ordeal whenever he had a tantrum. The therapist had to get the parents to accept the directive, and they would have a series of objections, which must be answered. The issue wasn't merely placing the boy in the room; it was having the parents agree with each other and jointly take some action for the first time.

"If he's stronger than you," said the therapist, "this is part of what we'll plan around. Because we have to have it work whether your husband is present at the time or not. So this is what we'll be working on. Even if your son doesn't like it, that's what parenting is all about."

"He won't go to his room," the father said. "I can't get him into his room."

"All right, now we need to find a place."

"There isn't a room," the mother said. "There isn't a door he can't break. He broke the lock off his door."

"We'll have to take measures," the therapist said. "This is so important that if we don't catch it now, and if we don't get it underway now and in the proper fashion, then it's going to get bigger. At eight he's a sturdy little fellow; at ten he's going to be that much bigger. As a teenager, he's going to be bigger yet. So it's important we stick to a plan. Can we strip his room down so that—or is there someplace else?"

"See, we're kind of crowded," the father said.

"I'm sure you are."

"Our house is small," the mother added. "If we put him in his room—well, if he wrecks his room, it's his room. He's going to have to live with it."

"So that is agreeable?" asked the therapist. "Would you both agree to his room?"

They both nodded, and the mother said, "The door is breakable."

"All right," the therapist said. "This is where we need to start taking extra measures." She turned to the father. "What can you do to reinforce that door?"

"Get another door," said the boy, but his comments were ignored in this conversation with the parents.

"The problem is," the father said, "he won't even go to his room. I can't get him in it."

"We'll take care of that in a moment. Let's address this."

"This all sounds funny," said the father, laughing nervously. "You're really serious about this?"

"I'm dead serious," the therapist said.

"You could get a metal door," said the boy, and again he was ignored.

"You know," the therapist went on, "what we're talking about is a temper tantrum that is already causing repercussions. And you parents are really obligated to help this young man."

"I guess I could pad the door so he doesn't hurt his hand when he hits it," the father said.

"Each time he has this behavior, this temper tantrum, you're going to put him in his room for ten minutes," the therapist said. "What we're talking about is 'time out.' It's a way to extinguish this behavior. Each time he has a temper tantrum, he knows what is going to happen."

"When he was younger, that's what we did," the mother said.

"Okay," said the therapist, "so we're really going back to that again."

"The problem is," the father said, "there's been many a time when I said, 'Go to your room,' and he won't. He just stays right next to me. I've tried to carry him up there, but he starts hitting and swinging, and I'd have to pick him up bodily. And if I do put him in the room, it's all I can do to shut the door. There's no lock on the door."

"Can you change that?" the therapist asked.

"I don't—it's hard for me to stand going through the scene of carrying him up and putting him in his room," the father said, looking sad. "It's traumatic."

The therapist smiled at him gently. "You know, you both came for help," she said. "And we can change this behavior and get this young man on his way. I don't know—are you sure you want him to get over it?"

"You're saying that's the only solution," said the father.

"I'm saying this week we've got to begin. You've tried a lot of things, and this way is how I would like to get to work this week. Now we'll be meeting in a week, and we'll see how it went. We can see where we need to go from there. But we need to start today. I may be wrong, but I thought that you said you were willing to get started on trying to make things better."

"Well," the father said, "I mean, we tried that same thing before. But you want us to do it again."

"In this fashion," the therapist said firmly. "Under guidance and direction. Then we'll be meeting in a week."

"Well, I'm willing to do it," the father said, "I just—"

"You're willing to change the lock?"

"I'd have to get a strong lock. He's got a little flimsy thing."

"The only one we had was broken off last week," said the mother.

"I can get a strong lock and lock him in his room," the father said, looking more determined.

"Okay, you know where you can get a new door if need be, or whatever," the therapist said to the father. "You can take care of that aspect of it. Each time it seems to be escalating into a temper tantrum, I want you to put him in his room for ten minutes. Now, when both you parents are home, I guess it's not as much of a problem, because you could take his legs and you can take the other part. The two of you can manage?"

"Oh, yes," the mother said.

"Right," said the father.

"Now," the therapist turned to mother, "the problem is when you're alone. Do you have a neighbor or a good friend that can come and help you?"

"There's one girl down the street who weighs about ninety pounds," the mother said. "In a real crisis I could ask her."

"This *is* a real crisis," the therapist said.

"Unfortunately, most of our neighbors are retired people. I really couldn't ask someone over sixty to help."

"Is there someone else, even the ninety-pound gal?"

"Yes," the mother laughed, "I could ask her."

"Okay, this is serious," the therapist said. "Now, every time he starts going into a temper tantrum, it's ten minutes in the room. If he comes back out and does it again, then he goes back into the room. The first time he may be in there an hour before he stops carrying on. He might be in there a long time before he can behave. But each time he does it, he goes back into the room."

"Okay," the mother said.

"I'll give you my telephone number at home in case you need to call me," said the therapist. "Feel free to call me. We'll meet next week. Now I would like to have you explain to Arthur so that he fully understands what is going to happen. Would you tell him that now?" she said to the father.

Even though the boy had heard the plan, it was important that he be told by the parents, not by the therapist, that they would follow the procedure. The father called the boy over to the seat beside him.

"Have you been listening?" the father asked.

"Yeah, and I'm tired," the boy sighed.

"For the next week," the father said, "any time you have your little tantrums, we're going to put you in your room and lock the door for ten minutes."

"Well, don't be surprised if I break the door down."

"Well, that's the procedure, you understand it?"

"Yes."

"Okay."

"And if he breaks the door down," the therapist said, "it will be ten more minutes."

The boy looked at her. "You want me to break every door down in the house?"

"We'll put up a new door, don't worry about that," said the father.

The therapist saw the family the following week and received a surprising report. The mother said that on Saturday
morning, when her husband was out on the golf course, the boy
had had a temper tantrum. She picked him up and put him in
his room. There was no lock on the door, and so she held the
door for half an hour until the message she sent to her husband
reached him and he came home from the golf course to assist her.

"Aside from that, which was early Saturday morning,"
said the mother, "we had a very pleasant weekend. One of the
best we've had in months."

"I'm amazed," the therapist said.

"I was, too," said the mother, laughing.

"Before I got there," the father said, "he had a big bar he
used for chin-ups that had rubber tips on either end. He had
been blasting the door with that. Both neighbors were wondering what was going on. My wife took that away from him. So
when I got there, I brought the punching bag in for him to have
something to hit."

"There was just this one time?" the therapist asked.

"Well, there was a couple of times when there was an ex-
change of words, but it wasn't any tantrum. I can't even remember what it was."

"It has honestly been the best week we've had in months,"
the mother said.

"Last night I was home alone with him," said the father.
He said to me, 'Mommy said if it's okay with you, I can go out.'
Well, he had stayed out the night before until dark, and so I
said, 'No, it's not okay.' He mumbled something about it and
said, 'Darn it, I want to go out, and that's not fair.' I just didn't
say anything. He eventually forgot about it. If that had been
last week, there would have been a scene about not being able
to go out. I guarantee it, without a doubt."

"I have to compliment both of you," the therapist said.
"Really, on taking this to heart and doing as fine a job as you
did this weekend. Hanging onto the door must not have been
easy for a whole half an hour."

"She was a wreck," the father said.

"And for you to hurry on home and get a new bolt or
whatever was necessary."

"Well, I calmed him down first," said the father. "Then I left and got the bolt and put it on. It was a big thick thing, but we never had to use it after that."

"I didn't think putting him in his room was going to be any big deterrent," said the mother. "Ten minutes in his room, from his point of view, I didn't expect to affect him. It might be a relief to everybody else not to have to deal with him. But he really resents it. He doesn't like going to his room, and he let me know that. Saturday morning when I was carrying him up the stairs, halfway up he said, 'I'll stop. I'll stop. I'll be okay now.' I said, 'Well, it's too late. You hit me and you're screaming at me, and ten minutes isn't forever.' But he ended up being in there closer to an hour."

"I have to compliment you for hanging in there. One of my concerns is that this is too quick."

"Frankly, I'm amazed," the mother said.

"You brought in to me a young man who cracked somebody in the nose, and this has been serious business. Now let's anticipate a bit, what could happen this next week that could really outfox you, or get you to give in, so that the plan worked out here might get sabotaged. See, we need to plan so that when you get into the heat of the battle—you did very well staying with it, but what could we anticipate might happen?"

"I don't know," the father said. "All this last week he's even been doing all his homework. That's a miracle."

The mother and father couldn't think of anything that might interfere with following through on the plan. The therapist suggested that father and son might do something nice for the mother that week to lighten her burden, and they decided they'd cook her dinner one night that week. That seemed a small thing, but later the father reported how impressed he was at how much work he and his son had had to go through to get it done.

The family were seen the following week, and all was going well. They discussed issues of organizing work in the house and the boy's progress in school. The following week they again came for an interview. Everything was going well again, and so the therapist saw them for only ten minutes. She

suggested they take the fee and go out to dinner instead of having an interview.

That was the end of the formal therapy. Telephone check-
ups found the boy behaving well. A one-hour follow-up interview six months later examined various aspects of their lives. The
mother reported that the boy was improving in school and had
a very nice teacher. She said the teacher wished the boy were a
little happier with school; in a class of eighteen boys she had her
hands full and couldn't help him as much as she'd like. The
mother also reported that the teacher and the boy had worked
out a plan together. "If he feels angry and can't function in
class anymore, he goes to the office voluntarily and sits at a
desk there. He works alone. That's satisfactory with his teacher."

The therapist said, "He has his own quiet time?" She got
up and shook hands with the boy. "I have to shake hands with a
young man who learned from his mother and father how to
handle tough situations and get out of the line of fire so he can
collect himself."

"He's been doing well in other areas besides school, too,"
said the father, and he described how the boy helped around
the house and took out the garbage.

"He takes complete responsibility for his own room," the
mother added. "He makes his bed every morning. He used to do
these things before at times, but now he does them pretty regularly."

They reported that the sister was doing well and was
standing up to her brother.

Summarizing, the mother said, "I think he's a lot happier
now, because he felt he could do anything he wanted to, even
though he was really suffering from what he was doing. I think
he was glad to know that his really bad behavior was not going
to be tolerated anymore. He never says anymore that he doesn't
like himself."

Later in the interview, the therapist asked the parents
what they thought had made the therapy successful.

"I was really surprised to get a solution," said the father.
"I've never had dealings with professional people, but I thought
it was all deeply theoretical and it was going to take a year to

pull an answer out of the air, and a team of analysts. I thought it was some real deep thing that went way back ten generations in the family, or something. And then your solution of putting him in his room and putting a latch on the door really surprised me. But we tried it in good faith, and it worked so well I couldn't believe it. It kind of restored my faith in being firm. I'd been trying to deal with my kids on the psychological level for years."

The mother said, "I thought it would be—I kept thinking there was something wrong with *me*. Because everything was going wrong, and I thought that after I changed everything would be fine. I was really baffled when we left here the first time. I was willing to try what you suggested, but it puzzled me. Because I thought it was going to be a kind of brain-picking session." She laughed, "All you said was, 'Well, things are obviously out of hand,' and I thought, you know, that's obvious. He has to be removed when he's like that. I used to tell him to sit down for five minutes when he was three or four years old, and I had stopped doing that." She went on, "We really had two sets of rules in the family. One was for everybody else, and the other was for Arthur. There was a tremendous amount of resentment. I was really puzzled by the solution, but willing to try it. I thought, why should he have a tantrum and ruin the whole family for the rest of the day? He should just be separated."

The therapist said, "It's nice to have parents who care enough to come off the golf course, and to go up in a nightgown and hang onto a door for half an hour."

"Boy, I'm sure glad that's over and gone," said the mother.

11

Pooping in the Pants

The parents were a young, middle-class couple very concerned about doing the right thing with their children. They were college-educated, and the father was a computer engineer. An attractive woman, the mother was keenly alert to what the therapist thought of her and how she was dealing with the problem. They had two children, five-year-old Timmy and three-year-old Billy. They were cute, active boys who quickly went to the wooden blocks on the floor in the family interview room and began to play with them.

The problem was Timmy, the five-year-old. He had never been toilet-trained. In fact, he had never had a bowel movement in the toilet, but only elsewhere. His brother had been routinely toilet-trained. Timmy simply did not use the toilet. As he put it, "I poopy in my pants, and when I go to bed, sometimes I lay down and poopy in my pajamas."

A brief summary of this case, without the recorded dialogue, was published in Jay Haley, *Problem-Solving Therapy: New Strategies for Effective Family Therapy* (San Francisco: Jossey-Bass, 1976).

The family had been seen for three diagnostic interviews by a child psychiatrist who concluded that the child needed extensive individual therapy. This problem of encopresis was considered a severe one that required extensive exploration of the child's ideas and fantasies with play therapy. After that evaluation, the family was referred to Dr. Curtis Adams for therapy. At the first interview Dr. Adams, also a child psychiatrist, asked the parents to describe the problem and what they had done to try to solve it.

The mother said that the boy would simply not have a bowel movement in the toilet no matter what was said to him or how often he was put on the toilet. She was constantly cleaning up his clothes. He either held back his bowel movements and went for days without one, which panicked her, or had several a day, which kept her constantly busy following him about to see when he had done it so she could clean him up.

"I started to get concerned when he was three years old," said the mother. "I asked the doctor about it. He told me to take it easy and not make an issue of it."

She described how "taking it easy" had had no effect. After that failed, she was advised to get firm and insist that the boy go on the toilet. She did so, and the boy responded by withholding his bowel movements. The mother said, "I began to get very concerned when he brought the constipation problem into it. By holding back, he could harm himself."

The father worked and went to school two nights a week; when home, he helped the mother clean the boy up. As he put it, "I always had the idea that these things solve themselves in time, but this one didn't."

The parents described themselves as somewhat divided about the issue until recently. "Usually I'm overconcerned," said the mother, "and my husband says there's nothing to worry about. That's our personalities. He tends to be the one who settles me down and keeps things in perspective."

The husband said, "I didn't worry about the problem so much. Live and let live. I thought it would go away by itself. Perhaps mothers worry more. But he is almost old enough to go to school in September. This is a problem. It could complicate him going to school. We thought something should be done instead of just letting it cure itself."

The therapist asked, "So you tried to solve it by being easy and by being firm. What else?"

The mother replied, "I would say to him, 'Well, you're going to sit there now until you do it. I want you to do it.' I showed him I was angry when nothing happened, which I hadn't been doing before. I put him on the toilet. He never minded sitting there. Sometimes I would give him a book, and he would get absorbed in the book. I even put the TV in the bathroom and let him watch, hoping that something would happen while he wasn't paying attention." She sighed. "But it didn't. Then the doctor advised me to ignore it, which I tried. It was difficult because I was training the younger one, so it was a problem to ignore Timmy while training Billy. We've just tried everything. We've tried being easy, being hard, and ignoring. Nothing seems to work."

The husband said, "The problem is my wife's during the day, but at dinnertime we always talk about it. He sits with us, and he'll look like he obviously has to go. He'll want to leave the table. What he wants is to go into his room in the corner and try to hold it back or get rid of it in his pants."

The boy, stacking up blocks in the corner with his younger brother, said, "I don't want to hold it back, just squeeze it in my pants."

"It is hard to ignore it," the mother said. "When he acts like he wants to leave the table like that, or he even says, 'I have to go do my poopy,' I rush him to the bathroom. Then he won't do it. The worst problem was when he started holding back. It would be days since he had gone, and he had a large one there which had to come out, and he wouldn't eat anymore. It took his appetite away. That's my impression. I would be pleased if he did it anywhere. But he just won't do it in the potty. He'll say no, or he'll change his mind completely about doing it at all. A couple of occasions, after he had gone to bed, he passed a big one which obviously hurt, because he would actually cry out."

The therapist said, "This has gone on for a couple of years, and it seems to have become the center of your life."

"That's true," the husband said.

"We've tried everything," said the wife.

"Well," the therapist said thoughtfully, "one of the things that concerns me is this: It has been going on such a long time, what would be some of the consequences of getting over it?"

"I think our primary concern is about him going to school," the father said. "If he can't go because of this, he'll be behind, and that would be bad because he seems pretty bright."

The woman turned to her husband. "I think that's a consequence if he *continues* with this problem. I think the doctor is asking us what happens if he gets over it."

"That's right," the therapist said. "What would happen if you didn't have this problem anymore?"

"I'd have a lot more freedom," the mother said, "because I wouldn't have all the extra wash and extra work. I wouldn't worry so much about whether we can go here or there, and what we'll do if he has one in his pants while we're there. Going out with less changes of clothes along would be great. We could go places we hesitate to go now. For example, we tried camping last summer. It created quite a bit of a problem because at a campsite there isn't much you can do with messy pants in the way of cleaning. I had them hanging around, and I had to worry about plastic bags and stuff. Instead of going through three or four pairs of underpants and long pants a day, as we do now, he would be able to stay in the one outfit from morning until evening. My attitude about him would change a lot."

"Well," the therapist said, "it's something to think about. We'll meet again in two weeks, since I will be on vacation next week, and we'll examine the consequences of getting over this for your family. This has been going on a long time, and when it goes away, it will make some differences. You'll relate to each other differently. You need to think about all those sides of it— the dark side, too. Let me leave you thinking about those consequences instead of going right ahead with the cure."

The couple and their children returned in two weeks. The therapist was prepared to talk about a number of consequences of getting over such a problem, since it had been decided with the supervisor that the strategy of the case would be *only* to restrain the family from improving. They were being required to go through the ordeal of having a therapist imply that they might not be able to tolerate being normal. He said to the parents, "What would happen in your family if you became normal parents? That was the assignment I left you with."

"We couldn't come up with any adverse effects," said the mother. "We just think having it solved would be wonderful. It's something that should have taken place naturally a long time ago."

"Yes," the father said, "we tried to imagine some of the possible things that might happen, and we could not."

"I see," the therapist said, appearing disappointed. "You must have thought about some of the obvious things that you might have to deal with if all of a sudden you were normal and everything was going well."

The use of the word *normal* was calculated. People don't like the idea that they aren't normal parents, and so they tend to react against the idea that they couldn't tolerate being normal.

"We could only think of good things that would happen," the father said.

"Fine, let's hear some of those," said the therapist.

"Well, we could go for rides together more often, things like that." The husband smiled. "Of course, I might also be tempted to stay away from home more. But I'm not sure I would, because I'm really a forty-hour-a-week man."

"Well, it's been forty hours a week plus school in the evening," the therapist said. "That means you have more drive than other people, and now that you've graduated, you don't have the school excuse for being away from home at night. If you didn't have to help your wife at home with the boy's problem, would that make a difference?"

"No," the mother interrupted, "my husband is just trying to dream up a problem because you asked him to. I can't see any bad effects from getting over it at all."

"Do you think your husband might work nights more then?"

"I don't think he would," the mother said. "He doesn't put in overtime unless it's necessary." She smiled. "But you know, now that the school excuse is gone, he's talking about going on and getting a master's degree."

"It crosses my mind occasionally," said the father, laughing.

The couple talked about the time involved when the father went to work and also to school and also raised a family.

"I think we'd go out together more as a couple if we were over this problem," the father said. "Now we tend to find things too hectic, and we say we're too tired to do this or too tired to go out tonight, and so on. I think without this problem weighing us down, we'd go out and do things together more."

"You could get a babysitter and go out and enjoy yourselves," the therapist said.

"Yes, part of the problem is a sitter," said the father. "Babysitters don't like the idea of changing messy pants all the time. So we'd rather not have that be a problem, and we don't get sitters."

"I see," the therapist said, "then without this problem you'd have to face the problem of choosing where to go out together, and all that, as normal couples do. You haven't had to face that."

"I think we could do that," the mother said. "In fact, we like to do things with the kids on the spur of the moment. But right now we have to pack so many clothes for Timmy. That can turn you off before you get started. Too much trouble, so forget it. I think that would change."

"What problems would that bring?" asked the therapist. "We're talking about what would happen in your family if you did not have this symptom. You'd have to go out more, you'd have to decide when to go, where to go, and who to see. You'd have to be more impulsive and just go somewhere."

"We both like to do that," the father said. "If it's a nice day, we say, 'Let's go down to the shore.' Without the problem we'd go earlier in the day and stay longer. That wouldn't be a negative thing if we were over the problem."

"Well, you don't know that, because you haven't had that situation," the therapist said.

"Well, that's true," said the father.

During the conversation, the therapist said, "One other consequence is that if a mother succeeds in getting over a problem like this with her child, she can be showing *her* mother that she's a better mother than *she* is. I don't know if that would be a difficulty you would have."

"You mean I might hesitate to let my mother know I have this problem?" the wife asked.

"No. If you got over this problem, it would be a sign that you're a mother who can solve problems. A competent mother. Sometimes a mother doesn't like her daughter to be competent and surpass her, and so daughters protect their mothers by not being very competent as mothers themselves. I wonder if you could tolerate being a better mother than your mother? That's what it might mean if your boy got over this problem."

The father said, "This is a different way of thinking. You have to put yourself in someone else's shoes and look at the situation more objectively."

"I want you to look at it more objectively," the therapist said, "and consider all the consequences of getting over this."

"I can tolerate being a good mother," said the wife. "I think what you brought up might be a problem, but only if I was closer to my mother. Actually, we're not very close. In fact, she doesn't like to visit and take care of my kids because of the messy pants."

"That would be a consequence, then," the therapist said. "There wouldn't be an excuse for her not visiting, and she might come and see you more often, perhaps even get closer."

"Well, she wouldn't *have* to come," the wife said.

"Would you visit her more often?"

"Probably," said the mother. "Usually if there is a visit, my parents come here instead of us going there, because we have the children to pack and all the clothes and all."

"So getting over the problem would risk getting closer with your mother. Would that be a problem?"

"I wouldn't mind being closer," the wife said. "Actually, if we were closer, we probably would discuss *her* problems, not my problems, since she prefers that."

"What sort of problems would your mother tell you about?"

"Oh, she drinks a bit, and my father has quite a drinking problem." The wife talked about her family at some length and did not seem to want a closer relationship with them. The therapist emphasized that if her child were not an excuse, she might have to be closer to them.

As the therapist talked, in a deadpan, benevolent way, about the consequences of solving the problem and whether they could tolerate being normal, the mother and father became increasingly irritated but continued to be polite. The therapist not only pointed out that they'd have to go out together as a couple and do more but added, "At the dinner table at home you'll have to find something other than this problem to talk about. As you describe it, that seems to be what you talk about from when father comes home right on through dinner."

"I think we would be able to find something else to talk about," the father said.

"Yes, really," the mother said, "pooping in the pants isn't our only subject of conversation."

The therapist emphasized the changes that would come about in their lives if they didn't have the problem. These changes were the ones that couples indeed face when they get over such a problem during successful therapy. By presenting these consequences to the couple, the therapist was warning them what they would have to face. He emphasized different areas: the change in mother's life—what would she do with herself if she didn't have that laundry to do? What would she think about if she didn't have this problem? He also emphasized the father/son relationship. Wouldn't the father have to do more with the boy if the boy didn't have messy pants? A primary emphasis was on the couple. Could they tolerate being normal parents and a normal husband and wife going out together and enjoying themselves?

The following week the parents were supposed to come back, but the mother called and said she would rather not come that day. Timmy had had a bowel movement in the toilet the night before, and she didn't want to "rock the boat" by coming in and talking about it. She asked for another week before an interview. The therapist agreed, and when they came in the next week, he found they had solved the problem.

"That Friday, for the first time, he did it in the toilet," the mother said. "He also did it Saturday and Sunday. Monday he didn't have a bowel movement at all. On Tuesday he had one in the toilet again. I just thought it was such a success that if we stayed away from therapy, it would give it a chance to settle into a routine."

"A good idea," the therapist said.

"He's been going ever since."

"Going regularly," the father said.

"The last two times," said the mother, "instead of us asking him, he came and told us he had to do it. Would we please put the seat on the toilet for him? That was the last two times."

"He hasn't soiled his pants in two weeks?" the therapist asked.

"Not at all," said the mother.

"That is really great!" the therapist congratulated them.

"It was almost as if he had to do it once to find out what was expected," laughed the mother. "For a long time I've thought, if he just did it once, it might do the trick. Once he did it in the toilet, that seemed to be it."

"It's kind of a sudden change," the therapist said, and he asked what they thought might have caused this change.

"We put some pressure on him," the father said. "I spent about half an hour in the bathroom with him on Thursday trying to persuade him to go. By that time he was quite constipated. It had been more than a week since he had gone, and we were afraid of the physical consequences. So we were at a point where we were going to have to do something to clean him out. It would have to be an enema, I told him."

The boy, playing with some toys in the corner, spoke up: "I do my bowel movements in my toilet now."

"Yes, you do," the father said, and he turned back to the therapist. "The threat of an enema was there when I talked to him Thursday. I let him try again Friday, before we were supposed to come here for our interview, but I went so far as to get the enema ready. At that point he obviously seemed to be weighing the choice between—well, I think between hurting himself by going, and getting the enema. I guess he decided that he was going to risk hurting himself. Once he did it, he was elated, and he did it again the following night. Then three nights in a row."

"That's great," the therapist said. "My only reservation is that this is too sudden and too much of a change. Is it possible you might need to have a relapse because it happened so fast?"

"That's possible, I suppose," the father said, "but I believe he really has been afraid to do it for fear of hurting himself. I remember he once passed a big one in bed, and he actually cried out because it hurt. I think this was on his mind. Once he did it without hurting, he didn't seem to be afraid to do it anymore. He seems to like the idea of going every day. Now he even tells us when he has to go."

"You feel you can handle him like a normal child now?" asked the therapist. "You don't need to go back the way he was?"

The mother laughed, and the father said, "Well, I'll tell you something. In just the last two weeks a lot of other things he was a problem about have changed. He's eating much better. The dinner table is more relaxed. I come home from work and my wife is more relaxed. There's less friction between her and Timmy. And we can talk about *other* things when I get home."

"So there have been a lot of changes," the therapist said.

"I think so. We're more relaxed about the whole thing."

"I certainly am," said the mother.

"I can see the change in her—she's not worried, so she doesn't quarrel."

"You really don't think you need to relapse on this problem?"

"I don't think so," the mother said.

"No," said the father.

"We have it behind us," the mother said, "and now we can do what we'd like to do."

"All right," the therapist said, pegging the change by shifting to a new topic. "Any other problems that concern you that you want to talk about?"

"No, I can't think of any," the father said. "But we still don't know why the boy had this fear. What do you think is inside him that would lead to this?"

"Well, he's normal now," the therapist said, "and I don't think we need to explain normality. I think we can move on to other things. I was really wondering if there are other family problems or marital problems."

"I don't think we have any," the wife said. "I think we've got a very good marriage."

"I don't think there is a problem," said the husband.

They talked about various issues that existed between them, but no particular problem could be formulated. The family was seen again for an interview two weeks later. The boy was over the problem. The couple said they were enjoying getting a babysitter and going out. The therapist switched to light conversation with the couple, and they talked about a beach they liked to go to and explained to him how to get there. In the process they became more equal to him, and he became less of an expert they needed to lean on.

In this case, the therapist had done nothing except talk to the couple about what would happen if they ever got over their problem. With this simple technique of implying that they might not be able to tolerate being normal, an ordeal for them, they recovered. In a follow-up it was found that the boy was continuing to deposit his bowel movements where he should.

12

Hitting Bottom

Raoul was a nice-looking young man from an upper-middle-class European family. His problem was a serious one: Every few months he became a bum. When George Orwell wrote about being down and out in Paris and London, he could have been describing Raoul, who had also been down and out in Montreal, Newark, and Madrid. Despite his youth—he was only in his twenties—he was experienced as a derelict in most parts of the world, having missed only the Orient.

Raoul followed a typical cycle, as if on a merry-go-round. He'd work hard, usually as a waiter, save his money, and live like a model citizen. After a few months, he'd start to spend his money recklessly, drink and take drugs, pursue prostitutes, and quit his job. In a matter of weeks he'd be without funds. At that point he would leave town and go on the road as a bum. Often he was hungry and could survive only by obtaining food at soup kitchens and skid row missions. After a few months as a derelict, he'd get a job, work hard, and live like a respectable citizen—until he quit his job and started downhill again.

When Raoul came to see me, it wasn't because he wished to get over being a bum. He wished to become a great writer, but he could not bring himself to sit down at the typewriter and write. He hoped therapy would solve his "writing block." Despite having considered himself a writer for a number of years, he had only a few pages of a novel to show for his ambitions. He had chosen me because a friend of his was a photographer who had been unable to take pictures and I had helped him solve that problem.

The friend had been trying to make a living as a freelance photographer, and he was talented enough to receive assignments from national magazines. Yet he would flub the assignments by blundering when taking the photographs. He'd leave the lens cap on, or he'd forget to load the camera, or he'd misread the light meter or in some way succeed in taking only bad photographs. These errors were costing him his photographic career, since his assignments were drying up. Largely by requiring him to make errors deliberately when taking photographs on an important assignment, the problem was resolved. He was required to leave the lens cap on purposely, for example, or to make some other error that would make him an incompetent photographer. With difficulty, he cooperated in that mad ordeal, and he stopped making errors in his photography assignments. Pleased, the photographer told his friends. Soon I was being visited by a variety of painters who couldn't paint, writers who couldn't write, and people who used being an artist as an excuse for not working for a living.

Besides wanting to be a writer, Raoul also said he wished to live a normal life. He wanted to give up his wandering like a derelict, and he wanted to have normal relationships with women. In the past his only contacts with women had been with prostitutes.

When Raoul came in, it seemed obvious he was about to take his plunge downhill again. Having worked as a waiter in an excellent French restaurant, a superior position in the waiting profession, he had recently quit that job in a fit of pique and was supposedly looking for another job. He was also spending the last of his money on elaborate furnishings for his apartment while saying that he didn't see how he could pay the rent next month now that he wasn't working. "After all," he said, "being successful as a waiter is not important. I am an intellectual. If I could only get to writing on my novel, all my troubles would be over."

"That might be so," I said, while thinking that Raoul was not going to pay his bill for the therapy interview taking place. Everything Raoul said indicated that he'd soon be on the road again and down and out in some other city. At the second interview, Raoul came in with an example of his writing, and I was surprised to see that he had talent. "I think you write well," I said to the young man, "and I think I can arrange that you follow a writing schedule. However, to be a writer of novels, you must have a stable life. It looks to me like you're about to wander again."

"I might not this time," said Raoul, "particularly if I get to writing and really start looking for another job."

I looked at him thoughtfully. "Would you like to know your real problem?"

"I don't think so," said Raoul.

"Your real problem," I said, "is that you have not yet reached bottom. I think you must keep going downhill and being a bum until you hit bottom."

Raoul looked relieved, and he laughed, "You don't know how far down to the bottom I have gone. Do you realize I have been literally starving a number of times? In Paris—in fact, in several cities—I was actually eating out of garbage cans."

"Everyone has a different bottom," I said, "and that was not the bottom for you. But let us talk of other things." We discussed writing and the kind of writer Raoul wished to be. He had the ideas, he said, but he simply could not sit down and write regularly. When he approached the typewriter, he became restless and got up to flee. Now, if he didn't find a job soon, he might have to pawn his typewriter in order to eat.

The following week Raoul did not appear for his interview, nor did he call to cancel it. He simply disappeared from the city, not paying his rent or saying goodbye to his friends. He vanished, and without paying my bill.

I received a telephone call from Raoul six months later. Having returned to the city, he wished to make an appointment to continue his therapy. He said he had an extraordinary story to tell. I said he was certainly welcome, and I could use an extraordinary story, as well as the payment of his bill. Raoul arrived and paid his past bill in cash. He was back at work and making good money as a waiter. "Let me tell you what happened to me," he said. "I finally reached bottom."

Raoul had left the city and hitchhiked across the country. In Albuquerque, New Mexico, he met another young man on the road, and they traveled together. They had no money, and they followed the not uncommon practice in the Southwest of sleeping in jails. A sheriff in a small town would let passing bums spend the night in jail and put them on the road out of town in the morning. When they got into the desert heat of Arizona, the two young men stopped overnight in a town called Dread Gulch. After hours on the highway without getting a ride, they asked at the local jail whether they could sleep there. The sheriff allowed them to do so. But early the next morning when they got ready to leave that town, the sheriff did not let them out. He put them in separate cells where they couldn't see each other. He said he would not let them go. Shocked, the young men demanded their freedom. The sheriff said they couldn't go until they saw the judge. When they demanded to see the judge immediately, the sheriff casually pointed out that it was Saturday and the judge was not available on weekends. Left alone in his cell, Raoul began to panic. He would be trapped in that small room for two days. Despite often being a bum, Raoul had never been in jail. In fact, he had an extreme fear of being in an enclosed place and being trapped there. One of the reasons he wandered was that he didn't like to be confined even in his way of life. Often he had found a city too confining, and now he was trapped in a small steel room, in the desert heat, for two days. Uncertain why he was being kept there and in a panic that he might never get out, Raoul almost went mad. He screamed and yelled, but no one would answer. What held him together was the idea that on Monday morning he would get free. He kept his sanity by counting the hours as

Saturday, and Saturday night, and Sunday, and Sunday night
went by.

On Monday morning, he told the sheriff when he brought
his gruel that he wished to see the judge immediately. The sheriff casually said that it was a holiday and the judge was not
available.

Raoul reported that he had gone out of his mind that
day. Helpless when faced with an indifferent and perhaps deceitful sheriff, he began to scream and lost all control of his
thinking. He saw the sun descend on his cell and fry him like an
egg, and he lost consciousness for periods of time. Whatever
structure there had been to his mind simply melted away. When
he was quite mad, he thought he heard, or perhaps he did hear,
a voice say, "You have reached bottom." At that point Raoul
recalled my saying he must reach bottom before he could
change. He immediately began to feel better and survived the
night without panic.

The next day Raoul was taken before the judge. He
learned that the friend he'd been traveling with was wanted by
the police in Albuquerque. That was why they had been held in
jail. Raoul was considered an accomplice of the other young
man. When the judge learned that they had met on the road and
Raoul hadn't been with the young man in Albuquerque when
he had committed a crime, Raoul was released. He immediately
took a job in a restaurant in that town, and he worked until he
had enough money to return to the city.

I accepted the fact that Raoul had finally reached bottom and so didn't need to continue his cycle of being down and
out. He could now become a respectable citizen, having survived that trauma. From then on the therapy was relatively routine. We focused on the three major areas in Raoul's life: succeeding in writing, being a respectable citizen, and becoming
involved with women in a normal way.

To encourage Raoul to become respectable, I required
him to do what respectable people did. Raoul had never had a
checking account in a bank, always living on cash. He was di-
rected to open a checking account. He was also required to ob-
tain credit cards, which he did with some difficulty, and to

open charge accounts in the local department stores. In that way he was placed in debt like other citizens. Raoul accepted all the tasks related to respectability. Instead of saving his money and splurging it, getting a job and losing it, he worked steadily and spent his money more leisurely, keeping regular hours. The question whether he should take or keep a particular waiter's job was defined in a special way. He had never liked the idea that he was a "waiter" and not a "writer." He was told he must find a job that would give him the most pay for the fewest hours so he could have free time to do his writing, which was his main interest. He obtained a very good job as a waiter in an excellent restaurant, where he made good money working only the dinner-hour shift.

Raoul had a mother and sister living in Belgium. His father was dead. Assuming that being a bum and not succeeding was related to his mother and sister at home, I began to rearrange Raoul's relationship with them. Raoul reported that he had an Oedipus complex and had been a disappointment to his mother. He had not been an army officer, like his father, or a prominent bureaucrat, like his grandfather. Instead he was a failure. Regularly he let his mother know he was a failure. When broke, he would always write to her for money, and she would know he was on the bum again. Often she would refuse to send money, but she would usually send it at the point when he was starving. He would then go back to work and not contact his mother while he was doing well. When a bum on the road again, he would write to her for money. Only when down and out had he ever written to her.

I required Raoul to write to his mother and his sister weekly. These could be polite letters that didn't say much, but they needed to be what a dutiful son would write. In some of the letters, he was to say he was doing well. Raoul objected, saying that if he established a normal relationship with them, they'd come over to America, and he'd have to live with them and support them. He was persuaded that he could avoid that eventuality if he put a little thought into it.

Raoul was also required to send his mother and sister a present. He refused, saying that writing was bad enough, but a present was too much. I pointed out that respectable people occasionally send presents to their families, and he should do that. When Raoul resisted, I said that he had to send them a present but suggested that it could be one they wouldn't like. Raoul agreed to that task. He spent days selecting the appropriate present and sent it off. His mother wrote to him, thanking him for the surprise present. She stated awkwardly that she was pleased but puzzled by the present. Raoul and I enjoyed reading her letter together, and after that Raoul was able to send his mother a present she *would* like. He also began to set aside money for a trip to visit his mother and sister—partly to prevent them from visiting him. He planned to go by air, staying at nice hotels in a respectable way.

Raoul's problems with writing and with women were dealt with simultaneously. In the sexual area, Raoul had a double problem—a physical difficulty and a romantic one. His physical problem was an inability to fully retract his foreskin, so that sexual relations were difficult. That problem was solved by the local surgeon in a minor operation that Raoul had been putting off for years. Once his equipment was in good shape, Raoul still faced a problem with women. He said that he had never in his life had a date. He had never been able to ask a woman out to dinner, to a show, or even for a stroll. Despite all the women he worked with in restaurants and associated with among artistic friends, he had no romantic or social relationships with women. He associated only with prostitutes. Raoul said that he had a block against asking a woman to go out with him. He just could not bring himself to ask for a date, far less attempt to seduce a woman.

I said to Raoul, "I can help you follow a strict writing schedule if you agree to do what I say. Suppose you were writing like a professional novelist, as you should be—how many pages a day would you write?"

Raoul speculated, discussed different drafts of pages, and ended up by saying he should do one finished page a day.

"How many words on a page?" I asked.

Raoul estimated 250 words to a page.

"How many days a week should you do a page?"

Raoul estimated six days, allowing one day a week off from writing.

"All right," I said, "if you really want to write a page a day, I will tell you what to do. Come to see me next week only if you agree to do exactly what I say."

With trepidation, Raoul said he would do that, but he would like a hint of what he was going to have to do. I would say only that the task would deal with more than one problem.

The following week Raoul came in and said he would do what I asked, since becoming a serious writer was so important to him.

"All right," I said. "Starting this Monday, you are to write one page a day of 250 words. By next Sunday you will have six pages written. If you do not have six pages written by next Sunday, then you have to begin telephoning and talking to women until you have three social engagements with three different women that week. These must be normal women, not prostitutes."

"Good God!" said Raoul.

"The following week," I continued, "you must write one page a day, and if at the end of the week you do not have six pages, then you must again contact three women and have three dates during the week. This plan is to continue until I change it."

"I would be scared to death to ask a woman for a date," said Raoul.

"Well, you have an alternative."

With this arrangement, one or the other therapeutic goal would be achieved no matter what Raoul did. If he wrote, that was achieving a goal, and if he did not write but had dates with women, that would be achieving a goal. A therapist wins either way with this approach.

Afraid of women, Raoul sprang to his typewriter and began to write steadily. As he got into a novel, he wrote considerably more than a page a day, but he always achieved that minimum.

After a period of time living a respectable life, having normal correspondence with his mother, and writing steadily,

Raoul came in and said he had been to a film the night before. This did not seem a startling event until he mentioned that he had asked a young woman to accompany him and she did. She was a bit mad, but she wasn't in the business of going out with men for pay. In the weeks that followed, he began to go out with other women, and he even became intimate with one. His female block, like his writing block, was disappearing.

I saw Raoul intermittently over a period of months, and his progress continued. Occasionally he drank more than he should, but not to the point of interfering with his writing or his job, and he continued to work and make good money. After a few months he decided to visit his mother in Europe. He thought he would travel there by way of the Orient, since he hadn't seen that part of the world. He enjoyed studying the travel literature and making his plans. Finally he took off and flew to Europe, staying at nice hotels in Hong Kong and Tokyo along the way.

Raoul stayed in Europe for over a year. He continued his writing and had his novel accepted by a French publisher. While finishing his novel, he returned to the United States and lived in a distant city. Occasional letters indicated he was doing well as a respectable citizen and a writer.

An Ordeal for Pleasure: A Story

Studying the red face above the clerical collar, Ian Wharf thought to himself that the priest drank more than he should. He wondered whether he should deal with the drinking as well as with the pleasure below the belt.

"You feel this pleasurable sensation every time you take a shower?" Ian asked.

"Not every time," said the priest. "I wouldn't be honest if I said that. But it happens just about every time. Now, Dr. Wharf, it isn't that I'm not supposed to feel the pleasure." In his distress the priest could still look condescending. "The point is I'm not supposed to *give consent* to feeling the pleasure. You not being one of the faith, I should make that clear."

"I think I understand," said Ian, "but sometimes you doubt whether you've given consent and sometimes you don't —is that right?"

"Lately it's happened so often that I rush through a shower as fast as I can. Yet I must give myself a decent wash. I've even considered giving up showers altogether. Never anything but a tub bath. But if I don't take a shower because I fear it, then I'm in sin because I'm fighting against seeking the pleasure." The priest's plump face was determined. "More than that, I won't run from the problem. It's there and I must face it. Yet as soon as that water begins to strike me down there and I feel that sensation, well—I almost go mad."

"I see," said Ian. "How have you tried to solve this problem?"

"Every way there is," said the priest with a gesture of despair. "Prayer mostly. Hours on my knees praying to merciful Mary to release me. I've even tried tranquilizers—a half dozen before a shower. But the doubt is still there—it's still there!" He struck the arm of the deep, comfortable chair. "Damn it, do I *seek* the pleasure?" Placing his fingers at his temples, he said, "Dr. Wharf, do you think I'm going mad?"

"No," said Ian.

"Well, that's a relief." The priest smirked behind his hands. "I've even thought of taking a knife to the problem. That's a mad thought, to deform oneself, and yet I thought of it." Sighing, he said, "Oh, I wish for old age and the end of such sensations!"

"What if the problem should become worse?" asked Ian.

"Worse! I dread to think about it. I don't understand why I have the problem at all, why it should strike *me*. But I suppose that's why I'm here—to understand it."

"I thought you were here to get over it," said Ian.

"Isn't that the same thing?"

"Not always. Now, I know you'd rather not think about it, but what if the problem should become worse?"

The priest looked at Ian as if seeing him for the first time. "I don't know," he said, "I suppose I'd wonder if I should be a priest."

"Ah," said Ian.

"It's been my life for seventeen years. I have no other."

"Mm-hm."

"Yet a priest must have control of himself. If I'm consenting to the pleasure, I'm sinning. Yet am I consenting? Perhaps I'm quite innocent. That's what drives me to the brink, that doubt. Can you help me, Dr. Wharf?"

"I think so," said Ian, "if you're willing to cooperate."

"You won't find a more cooperative patient. When the bishop said I was to see a psychiatrist, and one not of the faith at all, I doubted his judgment. Yet prayer has not helped, nor penance, nor even a long talk with the bishop."

"If I'm to help you get over this in thirty days," said Ian, "you'll have to do most of the work. It's the first of next month that you leave for your new parish, isn't it?"

"That's right, a promotion which I doubt I deserve. I'll refuse it, if that's necessary for the treatment."

"You're very agreeable," said Ian, with a calculated touch of irony in his voice. "The bishop wants you to accept the promotion; he feels you deserve it. So we'll see if we can't solve this in thirty days."

"It's a relief to hear you sound so hopeful, doctor."

"I can make no promises," said Ian. "But we might have a chance if you'll do exactly what I tell you."

"Yes, sir, anything."

"Fine. First of all, I'd like you to tell me in detail just what time of day you take a shower, how you proceed to wash yourself, and exactly at what point the doubt overcomes you."

Leaning back in his chair as the priest began to talk, Ian Wharf lit a cigar and studied its ash as he listened. Ian was a thin man who looked younger than his thirty-two years, and he liked to tip back in his chair and cross his legs as he listened to a patient. He would study his cigar, at times looking up to watch the eyes of a patient who was talking. He watched the patient's eyes largely with only one of his own because his right eye tended to roll about outside his control. He could see out of it well enough, but as a result of a childhood injury it would drift up and to the side and around while his other eye remained fixed on the person he was talking to. His patients appeared uneasy when they first saw the eye begin to drift, but they became accustomed to it.

As Ian listened to the priest, he wondered what he could do to help the fellow. The obsession was new to Ian, and he was still clarifying in his mind the difference between feeling pleasure below the belt and giving consent to feeling that pleasure. There was the rub—where the obsession could fix itself. Part of his mind listened for the technical details of the shower while another part of his mind drifted to his own problems with pleasure. Ian's doubt was the opposite of the poor cleric's—he wondered whether he gave consent to avoiding pleasure. Why else would I have married her, he wondered? With all the sensuous women in the world, I chose Lucretia of the long blond hair. Yet she had been sensuous. He examined the end of his cigar with his controllable eye as the perspiring priest talked on. The world changes, Ian thought. In the old religion, sexual pleasure could be a sin, and in the new psychiatric religion it could be a sin not to seek sexual pleasure. How determined we are to complicate our lives for no apparent purpose!

When the priest finally paused, Ian said, "I believe I have the picture," and he smiled. "Now, our goal, as I understand it, is to manage the situation so that you can take a shower without worrying about it, just like anyone else."

"That would be wonderful," said the priest.

"Fine. There is an essential first step. To succeed in this, you will have to do exactly what I tell you to do, no matter how silly it might seem to you."

"Yes, sir," said the priest. "What am I to do?"

"Don't be hasty in making this agreement," said Ian. "I want you to think it over for a week before you agree to do whatever I say."

"A week! But we have only thirty days."

"Yes," said Ian. "During this week I want you to take at least two showers and examine yourself carefully while you take them. I want you to have more clearly in mind—to the point of certainty—just when you have this doubt and when you don't. What I tell you to do will depend on your knowing that."

"Well, I suppose I can take two showers before next week." The priest looked carefully at Ian. "Could you tell me what sort of thing you might ask me to do?"

"No," said Ian, "you must agree in advance that you will follow my instructions without knowing what they are. Next week at the same time, then?"

"All right," said the priest.

"One more thing," said Ian as he walked the priest to the door. "I would also like you to think about what consequences there might be when you get over this problem."

"Consequences?" said the priest.

"That's right," said Ian. "Good afternoon." He shut the door, wondering what instructions to give to a priest who feared he was giving consent to pleasure "down there." He had put the man off until next week partly to commit him to doing what he was told and partly to give himself time to think of something to tell him to do. It will come, he said to himself, and he put the priest out of his mind for the week.

That evening in the kitchen, where they were having dinner because the dining-room table was piled with laundry, Lucretia said she wasn't feeling well. She suffered from a vague pain in her chest that she thought might be cancer. Ian tried to make light of it by saying, "In case it is, perhaps a visit to church this Sunday would ease your mind."

Lucretia stared at him with her pale blue eyes. "Your sarcasm isn't welcome," she said. "I can't help it if I have a pain."

Ian sighed, thinking once again that they were apart as if a plate glass window had stood between them. She knows it's there, he thought to himself, and I know it's there, yet each thing we do to reach out to each other only leaves the glass more solid. Yet she has been analyzed and I have been analyzed and the world has been analyzed, and all of us are in conflict, caught up in it like a web.

The priest came in the following week with a solemn expression for the occasion. "I'm prepared to do anything you say —but with one proviso," he said. "It must not interfere with my obligations as a priest."

"That's fair enough," said Ian, lighting up a cigar. "Tell me about the showers you took this week."

"I took two, and an extra one to be sure," said the priest. "The pleasure was there with all three, but only during two of them was I really in doubt whether I consented or not. The doubt came upon me quite early, before I had soaped myself. As soon as the warm water touched me, I felt the pleasure, and I did not know—I simply did not know—whether I consented to it or not. Each time the doubt ruined my whole day so I could hardly get anything done."

"Very good," said Ian.

"I'm glad you think so," said the priest.

"Ah, I don't mean it's good that you had the doubt, because I know that's distressing to you, but I'm glad you had the doubt so we can both get a clearer perspective about it. Now, you were also going to consider the consequences of getting over this problem."

"I've done that. The only consequence I can see is that I'll be a happier and better man and priest."

"Perhaps you haven't thought about it seriously enough," said Ian, looking doubtful.

"Indeed I have," the priest said.

"Have you considered the consequences with the bishop?" asked Ian.

"I see none there. He'll be delighted when I get over this."

"Of course he will," said Ian, "but he'll undoubtedly have other feelings as well. After all, he spent quite a bit of time trying to help you, didn't he?"

"Yes, he did, God bless him."

"After he did his best, if you come to me and get over the problem in a week or two, how will he feel?"

"I really don't know," said the priest.

"I think he'll feel a little put out at you and at me. He knows you well—he's your superior and your spiritual adviser. Yet you didn't recover when being helped by him, and you did when you went to a stranger."

"I suppose he'll feel that way a little." The priest looked puzzled. "But are you saying I should keep this problem because it might bother the bishop if I get over it, and him the one who sent me to you?"

"I'm not saying you should keep the problem," said Ian, smiling. "I'm merely pointing out there will be consequences to getting over it. As another example, when you don't have the problem, you'll have no reason to decline the promotion in a new parish."

"Well, I want that very much."

"I'm sure you do. Still, you wouldn't have to accept it, would you?"

"I could turn it down if I wished, but I should have advanced years ago. I don't know what my mother would say, she'd be so pleased."

"Ah, there's another consequence, you'd be pleasing your mother."

"Shouldn't I want to? She's been disappointed for years that I haven't advanced."

"Of course you should want to please her," said Ian. He added thoughtfully, "If it was necessary to disappoint her, you could find some other way."

"Disappoint her, indeed," said the priest. "I've devoted my life to pleasing her. I haven't even told her about the offer of a promotion for fear I won't be given it and she'll be unhappy."

"I see," said Ian.

"It was the greatest day in my mother's life when I became a priest."

"I'm sure it was," said Ian. "Well, I can see you haven't really thought about what will happen when you get over this problem."

"I hadn't thought of my mother and the bishop," the priest said, "but what else is there?"

"Oh, there are other consequences. For example, you'll have more confidence and be more sure of yourself."

"Heavens, man, that's no consequence. With this terrible thing on my mind, I haven't had the courage of a mouse. I'm ashamed to look people in the eye."

"Exactly," said Ian.

"I'll be able to hear a confession without feeling guilty about my own sins."

"Yes, that's another matter," said Ian. He leaned thoughtfully toward the priest, staring at him with his left eye while his right eye rolled slowly upward. "You and I are both in the helping business, and we spend our lives dealing with people in difficulty."

"That's true," said the priest. "We may go about our work differently, but surely we try to help people in distress."

"That's right," said Ian, "and I'm sure I don't need to tell *you,* but when we help people who are in misery, sometimes we find ourselves becoming arrogant and superior. We feel we're better than other people."

"That's true, it's the sin of pride."

"Exactly. Sometimes we are saved from that attitude if we have a problem we cannot conquer. A problem gives us humility."

"Are you suggesting I keep this mad thing I have about showers?"

"Not at all. I'm merely suggesting that it is no light problem to give up. Think a moment of the consequences. You'll no longer be a disappointment to your mother, with all the effect that might have on her. You'll have a higher status in the church, you'll be more self-confident, you won't feel guilty when you face the people who come to you for help."

"Really, Dr. Wharf, I think I can stand all that."

"I think you can," said Ian, "or I wouldn't have gone this far with you. However, as you change, you'll find it won't all be sunshine and roses." Ian set his cigar in the ashtray and sat back, folding his arms. "Now, are you ready to do what I tell you?"

"I am," the priest said, his face determined.

"Good. First, I want you to write to your mother and tell her you've been offered this promotion and you look forward to it. I want you to say that you're complimented by the offer and you're sure you can handle the new position. The letter must go off today."

"But what if I must give it up after saying such a thing?"

"Will you be saying what's not true?"

"No—well, yes. It isn't true that I'm sure I can handle it."

"What do you think your mother will reply?"

"She'll be delighted, of course."

"I don't think so. I think she'll write back something that puts you in doubt about your abilities."

"That's not true, doctor."

"I think it is."

"You have your opinion, and I have mine. I might add that I've known my mother somewhat longer than you have."

"If you express confidence about yourself in a letter to her, you'll find out I'm right. But I don't want to ask too much of you. Let me put it this way. You *must* write her that you have this new opportunity and you're pleased with it. Whether you say you're sure you can handle it, I leave up to you, in case you'd rather not risk it. Agreed?"

"Agreed," said the priest coolly.

"Now, then, for the showers." Ian leaned forward and stared intently at the priest, his right eye beginning to roll upward. "Every day this coming week I want you to take three showers—morning, afternoon, and evening."

"Three showers a day?"

"That's right."

"Isn't that excessive?"

"When you take these showers, I want you to examine yourself carefully to see if you're experiencing pleasure down there and to see if you're giving consent to that pleasure."

"I'll be doing that, all right."

"Now if, during a shower, you find you're in doubt about giving consent to the pleasure—even the slightest doubt—then you must do the following: You must step out of that shower immediately and dry yourself completely. When that's done, you must step back into the shower and turn the water a little bit colder. You're to take another shower, and if at any time you're in doubt, even the slightest doubt, you must again get out of the shower immediately and dry yourself completely. Then you're to step back into the shower and turn the water a little bit colder. You're to take another shower, and if you feel any doubt at all, you must do exactly the same thing again until you can complete a shower with no doubt whatever in your mind."

"God bless me," said the priest in consternation, "if I do that three times a day, I might have to spend the whole day in the shower!"

"You might," said Ian.

"This is asking too much, Dr. Wharf."

"Are my instructions clear?"

"Too clear."

"Then repeat them so we can be sure."

After repeating the procedure accurately, the priest said, "I may never get out of the bathroom."

"You must do the best you can," said Ian. "That's enough for today. I want to see you again next week at this same time."

"Now, look, Dr. Wharf," said the priest, "I didn't expect anything like this when I agreed to do what you said. What kind of psychiatry do you call this? I've read Sigmund Freud, I've read Sullivan. You're supposed to have me talk about things— my sex life, or where I learned about pleasure, and things like that."

"We have an agreement," said Ian, getting to his feet. When the priest reluctantly stood up, Ian added, "No one is to know about these instructions except you and me at this time. It's not the business of your bishop."

"I can't tell him why I'm so long in the shower?"

"It's your problem, not his." Ian walked to the door with the priest. "I know this is something you can do successfully. Until next week at this time." He closed the door behind the priest and turned to make his notes so he'd remember what he'd told the man to do.

The day the priest called, Ian had arrived home late in the afternoon. He was just settling down with his paper and a cup of coffee when the telephone rang and his answering service told him there was an emergency call.

"I think I'm going out of my mind," said the priest, his voice sounding far away on the telephone. "I didn't sleep at all last night, and now I have the terrible feeling I'm losing my grip."

"Have you followed my instructions exactly?" Ian asked.

"Exactly," the priest said, "and I don't think I can anymore. It's just too much. Yesterday I spent almost the whole day in the shower."

"You've given me your word," said Ian, "so I expect you to continue."

"Something is happening to me," the priest said. "Can I see you tonight?"

"I'm sure you can wait until our regular appointment," said Ian, estimating whether the priest could or could not. "I suppose we could arrange it, but I don't think it's necessary."

"I'll try to wait if you wish me to," said the priest, his voice trailing off as he spoke.

"Well, I have some time this evening," Ian said casually. "Suppose we meet at my office at nine o'clock and talk it over."

"Thank you, doctor, I'll be there."

Just before nine, Ian called upstairs to Lucretia, who was lying down, and told her he was going to his office.

"Again?" she said.

"This is the first evening I've worked this week. I won't be long."

"Is it really necessary?" called out Lucretia.

"Maybe," said Ian, "or maybe I just want to get the hell out of here," and he left.

The priest's hands were shaking when he sat down in the deep chair and lit a cigarette. "I've begun to doubt whether I should be a priest," he said, "and that's a terrible doubt." His voice had lost the semidramatic quality he had used with Ian. He sounded grimly serious.

"You see this?" The priest held up his quivering hand. "I haven't had a drink in two days, and I have the shakes. Not even a glass of wine."

"Oh?" said Ian.

"It's a mortal sin to kill oneself, and yet I've even considered that," said the priest, his voice assuming the more usual overdramatic style. "Will you release me from this agreement, doctor?"

"No," said Ian.

"Sometimes I think you're the devil. I've put myself in

the hands of Satan himself." The priest smirked. "I know it isn't sophisticated anymore to believe in the devil, but I'm not a sophisticated man."

"In my job as the devil," said Ian, "I would wonder why you don't drink to make this difficult period a little easier."

"That's the very point. *I don't want it easier,*" said the priest.

"Yet if a drink would make you feel better?" Ian said casually, knowing he'd save time if he blocked the priest off from drinking.

"I don't want to feel better when I have this problem," said the priest. "I didn't become a priest to have an easy life. I did it to sacrifice my life for God." He sighed and rubbed his forehead. "At least that's what I'm supposed to say, but I don't really know why I became a priest. It might've been a mistake. I might not be right for the calling. My father was a drunkard, you know. Oh, yes, and a violent man, too. How he beat my mother and how he'd beat me when he was drunk—if he could catch me! Yet when he was sober, he was the most quiet and pleasant of men. It just didn't happen often that he was sober. How my mother would plead with him! The more she begged him to stop, the more he drank, and the more he drank, the more she pointed at him and told me never to be like him. I believe she really hated him, or perhaps it was the drink she hated, since it gave him pleasure." He looked at Ian from behind his hands and smirked. "If you were a proper psychiatrist, you'd point out to me that I could develop a drinking problem because I identify with my father."

"Oh, you show more initiative than that," said Ian. "I think you could develop a drinking problem on your own."

"You don't mind if I say you're not a proper psychiatrist?"

"I don't mind."

"Do you mind if I say you have the screwiest right eye I ever saw in the head of a man?"

"I don't mind," said Ian.

"I can't tell whether you're looking at me or not. One eye points in my direction, but the other roams the universe. Can you control it at all?"

"Not at all," said Ian.

"How strange. Where was I?"

"You were saying you wanted to be like your father."

"I don't at all. God rest his soul, it doesn't matter now anyhow, for he's long gone. One night he was sitting on the edge of the bed staring at my mother. She was pleading with him to eat something, and suddenly he just lay back and was dead of a heart attack. A bit of vomit and he was gone from this world. I watched him go. When I realized he wasn't just passed out as usual, I was terrified. Bang, so quickly. My mother told everyone at the funeral that she had warned him many times about his heart. She had, too, I grant her that, and she had warned him about his liver and his spleen and every other vital organ. Doctor, will you let me out of this agreement? I simply cannot face that shower again tomorrow."

"No, I won't."

"You're a devil, not a man. You were right about my mother. I wrote to her, as you said. She sent back a letter, which I thought of bringing to show you and did not. She said she was delighted that I was getting my promotion, and the bishop would help me if I should begin to fail in my duties. She said she hoped I wouldn't drink too much and I would keep my health because it would be such a mark against me if the Church placed such a great trust in my hands and I failed. Tomorrow I'll get a box of cookies. Sometimes she treats me like I'm away at Boy Scout camp and not a man at all. When I was nineteen years old, she was telling me I was too young to go out with girls. Sometimes I wonder if she didn't encourage me to go into the priesthood so that she'd never lose me to another woman. That's a silly thought, I know, for she's a terribly devout woman. Well, doctor, this is a terrible thing happening to me, whatever it is. I cannot concentrate on my work. I cannot eat. I cannot sleep, and I simply cannot face that shower again tomorrow. Have you nothing to say to me?"

"I think you're doing fine," Ian said. "This kind of reaction is part of the consequence of going through a change."

"I'm glad you take it so calmly. A little sympathy would help."

"You don't need sympathy."

"Suppose I should go out of my mind?"

"I'll visit you at the mental hospital."

"That's kind of you. Will you cure me, too?"

"I don't think I'd need to. You'd cure yourself after a while, and you'd still have to take a promotion in a new parish."

"It's a heavy responsibility. Oh, I've known some priests who bordered on being idiots who had greater positions, but still it's a burden. My mother might be right, perhaps I'm not up to it. Sometimes I think I became a priest so that never, never again in my life would I have to take orders from a woman. Of course that's not so, but it's one of the merits of this life. Can we make it only two showers tomorrow?"

"No."

"Yesterday I hardly got out of the shower the entire day. I kept getting back in and back in all day. The day before was the same. I almost became waterlogged."

"And today?"

"Oh, today only the first shower was a problem, the others went more easily than I expected." The priest looked at him defiantly. "But that doesn't mean there won't be a doubt there again tomorrow."

"That's true," said Ian, "and you know what you must do if the doubt is there again."

When the bishop sat down to lunch with Ian, he put out his long, thin hand and said, "I'd like to congratulate you."

Ian took the hand, finding it cold. He could see that the bishop was genuinely pleased, yet behind the man's eyes there seemed to be a faint expression of resentment. "He's on his way?" asked Ian.

"Exactly thirty days after he came to see you. He's even confident he can do well in his new position."

"Let's hope so," said Ian.

"I don't believe I've seen a man so quickly transformed. What did you do in those few sessions?"

"He didn't tell you?" asked Ian. "I gave him permission to talk about it if he wished."

"He wouldn't say."

"Well, then, it's his secret," said Ian, wishing he could

talk to the bishop about it. "Let's just say he found a way to deal with the problem if it should bother him again."

The bishop smiled. "All he would tell me is that I'd put him in the hands of the devil." Watching Ian sip his wine, he added, "You puzzle me, Dr. Wharf."

"I'm complimented," said Ian. "I'm sure with your experience not many men do."

"I've known a few psychiatrists, and you aren't like them. You seem more like a surgeon than a psychiatrist."

"I'm not sure that's a compliment."

"I'm not, either," said the bishop, smiling. "But I'm grateful to you. This was a difficult problem, and I simply didn't know what to do about it." He watched Ian's right eye drift up toward the ceiling. Then the bishop looked carefully down at his hands. "I've heard rumors that—well, it's not really my business, but I've heard that certain of your colleagues have considered your methods of treatment a bit unorthodox."

"Oh?" said Ian.

"I only mention this because—if an issue should come up and you need some sort of testimonial, I hope you'll feel free to call on me." He looked quickly up at Ian's face. "I hope I haven't offended you by saying this?"

"Not at all," said Ian, surprised at the twist of uneasiness he felt inside himself. "I'm sure nothing like that will be necessary."

"I'm sure it won't," the bishop said, a faint expression of triumph replacing the resentment behind his eyes. "Do you like the wine?" he asked, and from then on the two men could enjoy each other.

Index